STYLEBOOK

FOR WRITERS AND EDITORS

EDITED BY ROBERT O. GROVER

DESIGN
Susan K. Langholz

PHOTOGRAPHY
Jeffrey MacMillan

U.S.News & World Report Inc., Washington, D

Printed on recycled paper.

2400 N Street, N.W., Washington, DC 20037-1196
Seventh Edition, revised 1994

This book was composed by the Composition Desk of U.S.News & World Report. *Printed in the United States of America.*

Library of Congress Cataloging-in-Publication Data
Grover, Robert O.—7th ed.
Rev. ed. of: U.S.news & world report stylebook for writers and editors/ Robert O. Grover. 6th ed. 1990
ISBN 0-89193-353-0 (pbk.): $10.55
1. Journalism—Style manuals. 2. Journalism—Terminology. 3. English language—Usage—Dictionaries. I. Grover, Robert O., 1942– . II. U.S.news & world report. III. Title: U.S.news & world report stylebook for writers and editors
PN4783.R6 1994
808'.06607—dc20 *93–31050*
CIP

• • • • • • • •

INTRODUCTION

We have aimed to make the U.S. News *stylebook as authoritative, easy to use and fair-minded as possible. Most of the entries provide cold, dry, practical answers to such value-free questions as whether certain numbers should be rendered in words or in figures. Other entries go to the heart and soul of a publication, encompassing everything from how to deal with quotations that include vulgarity and obscenity to how to handle language that reflects gender, racial, ethnic or religious bias.*

The stylebook is mostly nuts and bolts, of primary day-to-day interest to desk editors and proofreaders, but because it also helps set the tone for the magazine, it should be read by writers, editors, photographers, researchers, designers and illustrators alike.

Your comments and suggestions are welcome. Staffers may send them to Atex logon RG; readers may send them to: News Desk Chief, U.S.News & World Report, *2400 N Street, N.W., Washington, DC 20037-1196.*

ACKNOWLEDGMENTS

I am indebted to scores of people whose suggestions, support and gentle criticism helped shape this book and continue to keep it accurate and up to date. Special thanks to the members of the stylebook committee: Peter Meredith, Diane Javaid, Judy Shapleigh, Jim Sweeney, Ted Gest, Susan Vavrick, Kathleen Phillips and Michal Keeley; to Mimi McLoughlin, Mike Ruby, Kathy Bushkin and Karen Chevalier, whose encouragement and support were invaluable; to Sue Langholz, who made the book easy on the eyes; to Janie Price and her composition staff, who turned our mass of words into something typographically readable; to Jeff MacMillan, who captured so well some of the faces behind U.S. News; *to the staffers who let us use their faces and quotes to illustrate the book, and to the many editors, writers, fact checkers, researchers, proofreaders, librarians, artists, media colleagues, friends and readers of the magazine whose effort, influence and ideas did so much to make this book useful and this project a pleasure. They include, but are by no means limited to: Ed Albaugh, Dixie Barlow, Michael Barone, Gloria Borger, Elizabeth Brooke, Steve Budiansky, Tim Byers, Ken Campbell, Avery Comarow, Julie Corwin, Rob Covey, Susan Dentzer, Tom Dienes, Brian Duffy, Shirley Dutchak, Lynne Edwards, Mel Elfin, Scott Ellsworth, Charlie Fenyvesi, Kathleen Flynn, Kate Forsyth, Myke Freeman, Dick Gage, Joe Galloway, Dan Garcia, Don Gatling, Mark Godfrey, Norm Goldstein, Peter Green, Elizabeth Gross, Dorothy Grover, Wray Herbert, Kenneth Hooton, Robin Knight, Susan Lawrence, Susan LeClair, Virginia Lee, Cindy Leitner, Louise Lief, Lew Lord, Mary Lord, Pat Lute, Ric Manhard, Patti McCracken, Dave Merrill, Julie Nathanson, Cindy Phelps, Penny Pickett, John Plunkett, Doug Podolsky, Mary Beth Protomastro, Lee Rainie, Lesley Rogers, Tom Shantz, Joe Shapiro, Jeffery Sheler, Allan Siegal, Vic Sussman, Cathy Sweeney, John Walcott, Deborah Wallis and Len Wiener.*

Robert O. Grover

HOW TO USE THIS BOOK

Entry titles are alphabetized. For many questions, you can go right to the word or phrase you are seeking. **Connecticuter,** *for example, stands without elaboration, meaning that the usage is acceptable as written. For other questions, you might need to go to a general area. If you want to know, say, how to handle titles of cabinet officers, consult the* **titles of persons** *entry. If you want to know what residents of Niger are called, you can find it in the* **nations and regions** *entry.*

*Examples are in italic type (*Do it this way, if you please*). Examples that should be set italic, such as book titles, are in bold italic type (****The Firm****). Subheadings are all-caps lightface (*EXCEPTIONS*), and cross-references are in small bold type (***See fairness***). The electronic NAMES and PLACES files, which list people, organizations and geographic names in the news, are available in the* U.S. News *computer system, as is the stylebook itself.*

When a usage is proscribed, do not use it unless an exception has been agreed upon by top editors and the style editor. When an entry says a usage should be "avoided," don't use it unless you have exhausted alternatives. When several options are listed, use whichever one best suits the matter at hand.

For questions not explicitly addressed in this book, use analogy and, should that fail, use common sense in consultation with the style editor.

THE ELECTRONIC STYLEBOOK

Anyone with access to the U.S. News *Atex computer system can easily call up the electronic version of the* U.S. News *stylebook. In fact, many editors rely exclusively on the electronic stylebook, which has the advantage of containing all new entries and the very latest updates. Each chapter of the electronic stylebook is a separate file. To look up* **Mideast,** *for example, get the M file by typing "RE STYLEM-STYLE-USN," then do a search by typing "se [two spaces] Mideast." The NAMES file is "NAMES-STYLE-USN"; the PLACES file is "PLACES-STYLE-USN." If you have questions or problems, please consult any desk editor for assistance.*

A

'Everyone knows the truth hurts and then it sets you free, but is that with a capital or lowercase T?'

BRUCE AUSTER
PENTAGON REPORTER

a, an. Before a sounded *h,* use *a;* before a silent *h* and vowel sounds, use *an: a historic, an herb, an eye, an m* (sounds as if it begins with an e), but *a u* (sounds as if it begins with *y*).

abbreviations. Used judiciously, abbreviations save space and help speed the reader along. When overused, however, they can hinder comprehension and clutter type. Some abbreviations, such as *TNT, A.D., DDT, FBI, AFL-CIO* and *FM,* are better known than the words they stand for, and when the context makes their meaning clear they can be used without explanation on all references. Some others that are generally familiar, like *NAACP, NATO* and *NASA,* can be used on first reference in a tight lead but should be spelled out as soon as possible in a story. In most cases, the full name of an agency, organization or company should be used on first reference. Exceptions are noted under individual entries. If an abbreviation is unfamiliar, its first use should appear close to the spelled-out name so the reader can make the connection. Put an abbreviation in parentheses directly after the words it stands for only when a later appearance of the abbreviation would otherwise be unclear and when using the abbreviation is considered essential. For capitalization and punctuation, which often vary from one abbreviation to another, consult the entries below as well as entries for particular abbreviations in this book and in the dictionaries. **See acronyms, addresses, apostrophe, charts and tables, company, compass directions, initials, metric system, military titles, months, nations and regions, period, plurals, states, time, weights and measures and the electronic NAMES and PLACES lists.**

ABCs

ABM. Acceptable on second reference to *antiballistic missile. ABM treaty.*

abortion-debate terminology. Acceptable terms include *antiabortion activists, abortion opponents, abortion-rights activists* and *pro-abortion rights*. Except when we are quoting someone, avoid using *pro-life, right-to-life* and *pro-choice,* which are at worst imprecise and at best politically loaded. Don't use *pro-abortion* unless it accurately describes the person's or group's position. Don't use *pro-lifers* or *pro-choicers* except in quoted matter and then only when essential.

aboveground (adjective)

above-water (adjective)

academic degrees. **See bachelor of arts degree, doctor of philosophy, etc.**

academy. Capitalize in a name; lowercase alone: *United States Naval Academy (the Naval Academy,* but *the academy, a naval academy), the French Academy.* **See colleges and universities.**

accent marks.

acute: *Asunción, éclat*
grave: *Pietà, père*
circumflex: *château*
cedilla: *Curaçao*
tilde: *São Paulo*
umlaut: *Kurfürstendamm*

Substituting e for an umlaut (*Duesseldorf* instead of *Düsseldorf,* for example) is a style followed primarily by publications that do not use accents. Since we do use accents, we do not substitute the e. However, some names actually do use *ae, oe* and *ue* combinations, so we must be aware of the correct spelling. Correspondents should avoid spelling ä as *ae,* and so on, but indicate the umlaut in some way. Also, if a person really is named *Schoenhaus,* not *Schönhaus,* for example, the reporter should confirm that fact. Accents that are less familiar in the United States, such as Scandinavian, Polish, Czech and Hungarian accents, are not used in *U.S. News*. In headlines, captions and tables, except for capital letters and all-capital lines (as in photo credits), use accents as in body type.

accents. Do not misspell or put quotation marks around words that you regard as peculiarities of speech without a clearly compelling reason. The primary implication is derogatory, and, besides, the trouble might be in your ear. **See quotations.**

accords. Capitalize in an official name; lowercase alone: *Camp David Accords, the accords.*

Achilles heel. *Achilles tendon,* but in literal references, use an apostrophe: *"The head of the arrow for Achilles' heel smiled in its sleep."*

A

acquired immune deficiency syndrome. AIDS is acceptable on all references if the context makes the meaning clear.

acronyms are words formed from the first letter or letters of a series of words: *HUD* for Department of Housing and Urban Development; *LANTIRN* for low-altitude navigation and targeting infrared (system) for night. Write acronyms without points. Constructions that are not pronounceable words, *AAUW* (American Association of University Women), for instance, are abbreviations but are not acronyms. Plurals are normally formed by adding an *s: PAC, PACs*. See **abbreviations**.

act. Capitalize when part of a name; lowercase alone: *Immigration and Nationality Act (the act), an act of Congress, acts of Congress, Act I (the act)*.

active voice. In the active voice, the subject does the acting (*He opened the door*); in the passive voice, the subject is acted upon by the verb (*The door was opened*). Although there are times when use of the passive is preferred, such as when you don't know or don't want to reveal the doer of the action, those situations are few indeed. In most cases, the active voice, which is more vigorous, more natural and usually less wordy, is preferred.

act of God. As a legal term, it means an occurrence that is due entirely to the forces of nature and could not reasonably have been prevented. In nonlegal references, consider using the term *act of nature* instead.

A.D. Precedes the year; no comma: *bones dating to A.D. 357*.

addresses. Spell out and capitalize Street, Avenue, Alley, Route, etc., and numbered streets below 10 when part of a specific location: *Fifth Avenue, Coates Street,* but *the streets of New York*. Abbreviate compass points: *24th and N Streets, N.W.; 306 W. 42nd Street,* but spell them out in a street name when there is no address number: *Jamal lived on West 42nd Street*. Do not put a comma between the state and the ZIP code. When giving a complete address, use Postal Service state abbreviations; otherwise use the traditional abbreviations listed in the **states** entry.

ad hoc (adverb and adjective)

adjectives, multiple. Break them up. This sentence may be difficult to understand: *Farmers are planting from fence to fence to meet soaring world food demand.* Better: *Farmers are planting from fence to fence to meet the world's soaring demand for food.*

adjustable-rate (adjective)

administration. Capitalize in names; lowercase otherwise: *Food and Drug Administration, Grant administration, the administration*.

admiral. Capitalize before a name; lowercase otherwise. Abbreviate, *Adm.*, before full name; spell out otherwise: *Adm. Aaron Aument (Admiral Aument, the admiral)*. See military titles.

adopted, adoptive. Children are adopted; parents are adoptive. Do not identify people as such unless the information is clearly vital to the story. To indicate consanguinity, use terms like "biological parent" or "birth father" rather than "natural parent," which implies that adoptive parents are "unnatural."

adrenalin. Capitalize as a trademark for the synthetic or chemically extracted product; lowercase references to adrenalin produced by the adrenal gland.

adverb placement. The best placement for an adverb in a compound-verb sentence is usually where it sounds most natural, which more often than not is between the parts of the compound verb. In some cases, placement has no effect on the meaning of a sentence: *They have vociferously argued about finances. They have argued vociferously about finances.* In others, placement is crucial to meaning. In the sentence *Linda says she frequently finds misplaced gloves,* the finding is frequent. In *Linda says she finds frequently misplaced gloves,* the misplacing is frequent. See only.

adviser

affect/effect. As a verb, affect means to influence or to make a pretense of being: *How did she affect the outcome? He affected a nonplused attitude*. Effect, as a verb, means to bring about a result: *The movers effected a speedy transition;* as a noun, it means a result: *The music had a soothing effect on everyone*. Affect is used as a noun in psychology, where it means an emotion attached to an idea, object, etc.

AFL-CIO. American Federation of Labor–Congress of Industrial Organizations. The abbreviation is acceptable on all references. See union names.

African-American. See (-)American, black, racial designations.

after-dinner (adjective)

agency. Capitalize in a name; lowercase alone: *Central Intelligence Agency, Agency for International Development, the agency*.

ages. Use figures for ages of people and animals: *Susanne was 19 years old; a 5-year-old hamster; a man in his 50s; the police officer, age 27; the boys, ages* (not *aged*) *15 to 17; the 4-year-old was hungry*. Use figures for inanimate objects 10 and above: *the 15-year-old building, the five-year-old plan*. See **this week**.

ages and eras. Capitalize historical designations: *Stone Age, Dark Ages, Middle Ages, Jazz Age, Renaissance*. Lowercase contemporary expressions: *space age, nuclear age, atomic age, computer age*.

agreement. Capitalize as part of an official name; lowercase standing alone: *General Agreement on Tariffs and Trade (the agreement), the U.S.-Mexico trade agreement, the SALT II agreement of 1979*.

AIDS (acquired immune deficiency syndrome). Abbreviation is acceptable on all references if the context makes the meaning clear.

aircraft. For details, Jane's All the World's Aircraft is helpful. Note some cases in which *U.S. News* style varies from Jane's.
U.S.-MADE COMMERCIAL PLANES are usually identified by numbers or letters and numbers. Some planes also are given names, which may be used or omitted as desired. The maker's name also may be used or omitted: *Lockheed L-1011 TriStar (L-1011, Lockheed L-1011, TriStar), Boeing 747 (747), McDonnell Douglas DC-10 (DC-10)*.
U.S. MILITARY PLANES are customarily designated by numbers, with prefixed letters to indicate basic functions: A for attack, B for bomber, C for cargo, F for fighter, S for antisubmarine, T for trainer, etc. Often a letter is added at the end to show an adaptation or order in a series. Names, when they exist, may be used or omitted as desired: *F-4D Phantom (F-4D, Phantom), B-52H, C-9B, A-4, F-15A, S-3A, TA-4J*.
RUSSIAN PLANES are generally designated by numbers, with prefixes that are abbreviations of the makers' or designers' names: Tu for Tupolev, MiG for Mikoyan & Gurevich, M for Myasishchev, Su for Sukhoi, Yak for Yakovlev, Il for Ilyushin, etc. NATO specialists designate Russian planes with names beginning with F for fighter, B for bomber, C for cargo, H for helicopter, M for miscellaneous fixed-wing planes, etc. These names may be used or omitted as desired: *MiG-25 Foxbat (MiG-25, Foxbat), Il-76 Candid, Yak-28 Brewer, Firebar, M-4 Bison, Tu-144 Charger, Tu-26 Backfire, Su-19 Fencer*.

airfare

Air Force. Capitalize when referring to a particular country's organization: *the U.S. Air Force, an Air Force bomber, the French Air Force (the Air Force), the French and U.S. air forces, an air force*.

Air Force One

Air Force Reserve. *the Reserve, the Reserves,* but *reservists* when referring to individual members.

airline, air line, airways. The generic spelling is *airline,* but see individual entries in the electronic NAMES list for variations in company names.

air-mobile, but *1st Cavalry Division (Airmobile)*

airtime

Alabama (Ala., AL in addresses)

Alabamian

Alaska (AK in addresses; do not abbreviate otherwise)

Alaskan

Alberta. Abbreviate, *Alta.,* only in maps, charts and tables.

Albertan

Allah. See deity, Islam.

Alley. Capitalize in an address. See addresses.

alliance. Capitalize as part of an official name; lowercase in unofficial names and alone: *Alliance for Responsible Health Policy (the alliance), Atlantic alliance* (not the official name of NATO).

Allies, Allied. Capitalize only in a name or in reference to groupings historically known as *the Allies,* the nations that opposed Germany in World Wars I and II. Lowercase otherwise, as when applied to partners of the United States or to allies of any nation. Do not capitalize allies or allied when referring to NATO: *The Allies defeated the Central Powers in 1918 (the Allies); the Allied debacle at the Somme; the NATO allies (the allies); allies of the United States in NATO; U.S. allies in Europe and Asia*.

all out (adverb): *to go all out; all-out* (adjective): *an all-out effort.*

all right (adverb): *Everything is all right; all-right* (adjective): *He's an all-right guy.*

almanacs, names of. Set roman, no quotes. See book titles.

alternate/alternative. As an adjective, alternate means every other: *Meetings were held on alternate Sundays*. Alternative as a noun means a choice between two or more things: *An alternative to the church was the school;* as an adjective, it also means appealing to the unconventional: *The dropouts published an alternative newspaper.*

A

a.m. See time.

ambassador. Capitalize with a name; lowercase otherwise: *Ambassador Marcus Brine (Ambassador Brine), the U.S. ambassador to Switzerland, the ambassador.*

amendment. Capitalize in a name; lowercase otherwise: *Fifth Amendment, 14th Amendment, the amendment, an amendment, Maryland's Equal Rights Amendment* (it is in effect), but *federal equal rights amendment* (it has not been adopted).

(-)American. Hyphenate ethnic combinations: *Irish-American, Italian-American, Mexican-American, African-American,* but *Latin American*.

AM/FM-cassette player

ampersand (&). Use for *and* in company and firm names, even when the company prefers to use *and*. Use *and* in names of governmental units, unions and trade, nonprofit and professional groups. Write abbreviations without spaces: *R&D, B&B*.

anointing of the sick. See sacraments.

another. Don't use *another* when you mean *an additional: They borrowed $500. They borrowed another $500. They borrowed an additional $1,500,* or *They borrowed $1,500 more.*

Antarctic, *Antarctica, the Antarctic, Antarctic Ocean*

ante( ). Generally solid except before an e or a capitalization or in classical expressions: *antecedent, antemeridian,* but *ante meridiem* (a.m.).

anti( ). Solid except before *i* or a capitalization or in confusing made-up combinations and words hyphenated by the dictionary: *antiabortion, antiapartheid, antiaircraft, antiballistic missile, anti-intellectualism, anti-American, anti-bias, anti-union, anti-dumping.*

antiballistic missile system

antiballistic missile treaty. *ABM treaty* is acceptable on second reference.

anti-Christ. An opponent of or disbeliever in Christ.

Antichrist. The biblical antagonist of Christ.

antisemitic describes persons who discriminate against or persecute Jews. Do not use for Jews or gentiles who oppose Israeli policies.

anymore (adverb): nowadays, at present; *any more:* anything additional.

anyplace (adverb): *can't go anyplace,* but *in any place, to any place.*

anytime or *at any time*

apostrophe. POSSESSIVES OF SINGULAR WORDS are normally formed by adding *'s: a man's home, James's friend, Los Angeles's weather, Jesus's teachings.* IN SOME SET EXPRESSIONS, especially before the word *sake,* only an apostrophe is used to form the possessive: *for goodness' sake, for convenience' sake.* POSSESSIVES OF PLURAL WORDS that have become plural by addition of s or es are formed by an apostrophe only: *leaders' views, the Joneses' house, General Motors' parking lot, the United States' viewpoint.*
POSSESSIVES OF ITALICIZED WORDS should be avoided by writing around them. If you must use one, romanize the *'s: the* ***Times****'s opinion.*
FOR PLURALS OF LETTERS, use s when it's clear *(GIs, HMOs)*. Use 's when it would be confusing if s alone were added *(SOS's),* with single letters *(S's, A's),* with lowercase letters used as nouns *(x's and y's)* and in abbreviations with periods *(M.A.'s).*
FOR PLURALS OF NUMBERS, add only s*: F-16s, 1990s, the '30s.*
IN PLURALS OF PROPER NAMES, do not use an apostrophe or alter spelling: *all the Marys, two Germanys, 1957 Pontiacs.*
IN THE NAME OF A COMPANY, association, union, government agency or military unit, if the official name omits an apostrophe, follow that style: *Reserve Officers Training Corps.*
IN GERUND CONSTRUCTIONS (where a verb is used as a noun), use an apostrophe: *The Secret Service would not hear of the president's going out alone.* A test of this construction: You would not write: "I will not hear of him going out alone." You would write: "I will not hear of his going out alone." If the language becomes confusing or too complicated, consider rewriting.
FOR TRAVEL TIME, use a hyphen construction or an apostrophe construction, but do not mix them: *a two-hour flight* or *a two hours' flight* but not *a two-hours' flight.*
JOINT POSSESSION. When ownership is joint, use an apostrophe only with the last owner (*Bill and Julie's children*); when ownership is individual, use an apostrophe after all owners (*Bill's and Julie's underwear*). See double genitive, plurals.

appendix. Capitalize as in *Appendix A;* lowercase when alone.

April. Do not abbreviate except in charts and tables. See dates, months.

Arabic names. Confusion arises over spelling and what parts of a name to use, especially on second reference. Variations have grown out of Western efforts to reproduce Arabic sounds: A French administrator might spell a name with an *-oun* and an American reporter with a *-un* or a *-ur,* depending on the writer's ear and education. Some frequently used Arabic names have acquired generally accepted spellings, and a number of Arabs westernize their names. Their preferences should be followed. Where neither a personal preference nor an agreed spelling exists, use the system of transliteration devised by the Library of Congress. Ignore the

apostrophelike marks and the hyphens before *al*. In most cases, use only the last word of a name in subsequent references.
SAUDI PRINCES are known by their first names: *Prince Bandar ibn Abdul-Aziz (Prince Bandar, Bandar)*.
BREAKDOWN. *Gamal Abdel Nasser* was formed as follows: *Gamal* (the individual's name) *Abd al-Nasir* (father's name). *Abd al-Nasir* comes from *Abd* (worshiper of) *al* (the) *Nasir* (Victorious One—one of the names of God). Sometimes a grandfather's name or a family name is added. Sometimes a particle meaning *son of* or *daughter of* is inserted before the father's name and the grandfather's name: *ibn, bin, ben* (son of); *bint* (daughter of). Spell it *ibn* unless another spelling is firmly established. Lowercase when preceded by other parts of the name; capitalize when it is the first part used: *Ibn Saud*. "The" appears as *al, el, ed, as, ud, ul, ur*. Unless usage or individual preference dictates otherwise, use it only with a full name, spell it *al* and connect it with a hyphen to the following word.
GENERAL RULES. Follow the spellings in the electronic NAMES list, then in Webster's New World Dictionary and Webster's Biographical Dictionary. If the individual has westernized the name, use that spelling, and use the name the individual elects for subsequent mention unless it is too cumbersome. In the absence of a known preference, use the established form and spelling. If there is disagreement about form or spelling, get as close as possible to standard press practice.
HELP WITH QUESTIONS: An Arabic-speaking writer on the staff; Near East Section, Library of Congress; Foreign Service Institute of the State Department; country desks of the State Department; press officers of Arab diplomatic missions.

arabic numerals. See numbers.

arch( ). Solid except before capitalization: *archenemy*.

Arctic, *the Arctic, Arctic Circle,* but lowercase *arctic* when merely describing very cold conditions.

areas with special and familiar names. See locations.

Arizona (Ariz., AZ in addresses)

Arizonan

Arkansan

Arkansas (Ark., AR in addresses)

Armistice Day is now called Veterans Day.

Army. Capitalize when referring to a specific country's organization and when part of the name of a unit; lowercase standing alone in reference to a unit: *the U.S. Army (the Regular Army, the all-volunteer Army, the Army), the Russian Army (the*

Army), the U.S. and Russian armies, an army, the 7th Army (the army).

Army Reserve. *the Reserve, a Reserve major, the Reserves,* but *reserves* and *reservists* when referring to individual members.

Article. Capitalize as in *Article III of the Constitution;* lowercase alone: *the article.*

articles, titles of. Use quotation marks. See titles of works.

Asian is generally preferred to *Oriental* for references to people.

assembly. Capitalize when referring to the United Nations General Assembly, to a country's national assembly or to a state's general assembly: *the Indiana General Assembly (the General Assembly, the Assembly), the Oregon Legislative Assembly, the assemblies of Indiana and Kentucky, the French National Assembly (the National Assembly, the Assembly).*

associate justice. *Associate Justice* is the formal title of Supreme Court justices other than the chief justice, but *Justice* is an acceptable alternative. Capitalize before a name; lowercase alone: *Associate Justice Sandra Day O'Connor (Justice Sandra Day O'Connor, Justice O'Connor, the associate justice, the justice).*

association. Capitalize in a name; lowercase alone: *the National Association of State Development Agencies (the association), Pulaski Savings & Loan Association (the association).* The abbreviation, *Assn.,* may be used in charts and tables.

at large. Do not hyphenate as a title; hyphenate when used adjectivally: *Delegate at Large Stegman, the delegate at large, the delegate-at-large election.*

attorney, U.S. Capitalize before a full name; lowercase otherwise: *U.S. Attorney Anna Basham (the U.S. attorney).*

attorney general (attorneys general). Capitalize before a name; lowercase otherwise. Do not abbreviate: *Attorney General Roy Vondy, the attorney general.*

audiocassette

audiotape

auger/augur. An auger is a tool. As a noun, augur is a prophet; as a verb, it means to prophesy.

August. See dates, months.

auto driver, *auto maker, auto repairman, auto worker*

automobiles. *two-door sedan, V-8, the car has six cylinders, a six-cylinder engine*.

Avenue. Capitalize when part of an address. Do not abbreviate. See addresses.

AWACS (airborne warning and control system) planes. Boeing E-3A.

awhile. *They played awhile,* but *They played for a while*.

ax, axes

B

'I came to U.S. News *as a summer intern to learn about the business. I have stayed because I continue to be introduced to new and exciting aspects of journalism.'*

ALEJANDRO BODIPO-MEMBA
RESEARCHER

B-1B (B-1Bs). See aircraft.

baby boom, *baby boom generation, baby boomer*

baby-sit (verb), *baby sitter* (noun), *baby-sitting* (noun and adjective)

bachelor of arts degree (B.A. or A.B.), *bachelor's degree, bachelor's*

bachelor of science degree (B.S.), *bachelor's degree, bachelor's*

backcountry

back door (noun), *backdoor* (adjective)

backdown (noun), *back down* (verb)

back fence (noun), *back-fence* (adjective)

backflash

backflow

backslash (noun). A reverse virgule.

back stairs (noun), *backstairs* (adjective)

back track (noun), *backtrack* (verb)

back up (verb), *backup* (noun and adjective)

back yard (noun), *backyard* (adjective)

back yard, America's. Many people find some uses of this expression objectionable, contending that it implies a patronizing attitude toward neighbors of the United States, so use the term advisedly, if at all.

bacteria. The singular is *bacterium*. Don't write *a bacteria*.

Bangladeshi(s). Citizen of Bangladesh. Use *Bengali* in references to Bengali-speaking residents of Bangladesh and India.

baptism

Baptists. Four major divisions are the Southern Baptist Convention; the National Baptist Convention, U.S.A. Inc.; the National Baptist Convention of America, and the American Baptist Churches in the U.S.A. Refer to Baptist groups by name; it is incorrect to write "the Baptist church" except in reference to a local congregation. Baptist groups do not have bishops, but they have a structure of boards and agencies at various levels. Use of the term "Reverend" is problematic among Baptists. It is best to avoid titles. Although deacons are ordained to assist pastors and do similar work, they are laypersons, not members of the clergy. The organizational structure of each group is somewhat different, but terminology is similar: *Southern Baptist Convention (the convention, the denomination); First Baptist Church (the church); John J. Pomeroy, pastor of the First Baptist Church (the pastor, Pomeroy or John J. Pomeroy, a Baptist minister or clergyman); John J. Pomeroy, a deacon in the First Baptist Church (the deacon, Pomeroy)*.

baron, baronet. See nobility.

baroque. Capitalize when referring to the specific style of art and architecture that flourished from 1600 to 1750; lowercase in generic references: *a Baroque opera, the skateboard's baroque design*.

barrel(s). Use abbreviation, *bbl.*, only in charts, maps and tables.

Bastille Day

battalion. Capitalize when part of a name; lowercase alone: *4th Battalion (the battalion, the battalion commander)*.

battle cruiser

battlefront

battle-wise

bay. Capitalize when part of a name; lowercase otherwise: *Mobjack Bay (the bay)*.

BBC. When clear, acceptable on first reference to British Broadcasting Corp.

B.C. Follows year or century; no comma: *painted in 2500 B.C.*

bear market (noun), *bear-market* (adjective)

bed and breakfast (noun); *bed-and-breakfast* (adjective). *B&B* is acceptable on second reference when the meaning is clear.

belt. Capitalize in combinations for such recognizable areas as Corn Belt, Cotton Belt and Sun Belt, but lowercase *rust belt* (and similar terms) because there is no consensus on its boundaries. See Bible Belt.

belt tightening (noun), *belt-tightening* (adjective)

beltway. Capitalize in names: *Capital Beltway, Baltimore Beltway;* lowercase alone: *cruising the beltway, an inside-the-beltway mentality*.

benchmark. A standard in measuring quality or value; *bench mark:* a surveyor's mark made on a permanent landmark.

bestseller (noun and adjective), *bestselling*

between/from. Use *and* with *between: They shoot between 50 and 250 rounds daily.* Use *to* with *from: They shoot from 50 to 250 rounds daily.*

bi( ). Combines solid except before a capitalized word or *i*.

biannual. Use it to mean semiannual, twice a year. For every two years, write *biennial*.

bias. See epithets, ethnic identification, fairness, gender bias, he/she, man and racial designations.

Bible, the. Capitalize, but lowercase in figurative sense: *the volleyballers' bible*.

Bible Belt can be offensive to many people, so use it with care.

biblical references. In citing passages from the Bible, use book, chapter and verse (roman type, no abbreviations): *2 Chronicles 7:14; Proverbs 3:5-6; Psalms 23:1-6,* but *the 23rd Psalm.*

biennial. Every two years. For twice a year, write *biannual* or *semiannual.*

big government

Big Two (Three, Four, etc.). Use expressions like *Big Oil* only when the article makes quite clear what is meant.

bil. Acceptable for *billion(s)* in charts, maps and tables.

bill. Lowercase for legislation, even when used with popular names that are capitalized because they might be unclear in themselves: *clean-air bill, Levin-Mikulski bill, the Sunshine in Government bill,* but *GI Bill, Bill of Rights.*

billion. See million.

Bill of Rights

bimonthly. Once every two months. For twice a month, write *semimonthly.*

birthrate

bishop. Capitalize before a name; lowercase otherwise: *Bishop George Manship (Bishop Manship, the bishop), Suffragan Bishop George Manship (the suffragan bishop).*

biweekly. Once every two weeks. For twice a week, write *semiweekly.*

black. African-American, Afro-American and black are acceptable as synonyms, but take personal preference into account when applying the terms to individuals. See racial designations.

black caucus, but *Congressional Black Caucus*

Black Muslim should be used only as a historical term or when quoting someone. See Islam, Muslim.

blastoff (noun), *blast off* (verb)

blond (noun and adjective, male and female)

blue book. An official government report or a social registry; *bluebook:* a student examination booklet.

blue ribbon (noun), *blue-ribbon* (adjective)

board. Capitalize in a name; lowercase alone: *Federal Reserve Board (the board), the Lynn County Board of Regents, the Board of Regents, a board of regents.*

B

boatlift (noun). A system of moving people by boat.

boat lift (noun). A device that raises boats from the water.

boatyard

bobby socks (noun)

bobby-sox (adjective), *bobby-soxer* (noun)

Bohemian. Capitalize in references to Bohemia; lowercase in references to lifestyle.

book titles. Set in italics, and capitalize the title as the book does, except when the title is in all caps or all lowercase, in which case capitalize only principal words and prepositions and conjunctions of more than three letters. For well-known standard reference works, like almanacs, dictionaries and encyclopedias, and religious books, like the Bible and the Koran, use roman type, with no quotation marks. Do not use a comma between a book title and the author's name: ***The Bonfire of the Vanities*** *by Tom Wolfe.* Initial articles may be dropped if the syntax would make a sentence awkward: *The film was not faithful to Wolfe's* ***Bonfire of the Vanities.*** See titles of works.

boomtown

bond ratings. *AAA, AA, A, BBB, BB,* etc.

border states. See political regions.

( )bound. Combinations are generally solid, but hyphenate when used with a proper noun: *leatherbound, snowbound, deskbound, dutybound, homewardbound, westbound, Washington-bound.*

box office (noun and adjective)

boy. Do not use for males 18 and older.

brackets. Use brackets for parenthetical material within parentheses and to enclose explanatory matter that the magazine inserts in letters to the editor, exact texts or quoted passages: *"He stayed through the final meeting [March 26, 1977] before flying home."* See parentheses.

brain trust, *brain truster*. Lowercase general references, but capitalize in references to Franklin Roosevelt's advisory group.

brainwash, *brainwasher, brainwashing*

brand names. See trademarks.

Brazilian names. Names of Brazilians generally resemble those of the Portuguese. But, because of Brazil's polyglot culture, even more caution is indicated in determining individual usage. If there are doubts about whether to use both parts of a double surname, it is safer to do so. *João Baptista Pinheiro (Pinheiro); Francisco Thompson Flores Neto (Thompson Flores)*. *Neto* is not a basic part of the name but an appendage that means grandson. *Maria Regina Breves Barringer (Barringer)*.

British Columbia. Abbreviate, *B.C.,* only in charts, maps and tables.

British Columbian

British spellings. Use U.S. spellings for generic words that are part of proper names unless the British spelling is also used in America as an alternative spelling: *the British Labor Party, Britain's Ministry of Defense,* but *the Barbican Centre*.

British thermal unit. See Btu.

brokerage means "the business or office of a broker," so *brokerage firm* is redundant.

Brothers. In company names, capitalize and spell out or abbreviate as the company does. *Bro.* and *Bros.* are acceptable in charts and tables.

brunet (noun and adjective, male and female)

brush fire (noun), *brush-fire* (adjective)

brussels sprouts

Btu. Abbreviation for British thermal unit, acceptable on all references when the meaning is clear: *25 Btu, a 500-Btu air conditioner*.

budget, federal

Budget Message. Capitalize when referring to the U.S. president's message.

buildings. Capitalize names: *the Empire State Building; his home, Dunrovin; the Zambian Embassy (the embassy); the U.S. Capitol (the Capitol)*.

bull market (noun), *bull-market* (adjective)

bus (buses)/**buss** (busses). A bus is a vehicle; buss is a kiss or to kiss.

businessman, businesswoman, but *small-business man*. Consider using gender-neutral alternatives, like *businessperson, businesspeople, business executive*.

( )buster. Write solid: *broncobuster, crimebuster, trustbuster, budgetbuster*.

buyback

buyer's market

bylines. In "up" style bylines, lowercase *with,* the rule on headline capitalization notwithstanding. For byline spelling and initials, follow the masthead; for stringers' names, consult the STRINGERS file in BBD-USN. Sign editors' notes —***The Editors*** in italics at the end of the note. When the signature is on a line by itself, set it flush right. When using initials as a story credit, use a dash, periods and no spaces between the end of the text and the initials or between the initials themselves:—*R.J.N.*

Byzantine. Capitalize references to Byzantium or the Byzantine Empire; lowercase references to complex or devious political situations.

C

'From the temples of Tikal to the back porches of Mill City, Ore., what a job!'

BETSY CARPENTER
ENVIRONMENTAL REPORTER

cabinet. Lowercase all uses. See department.

cabinet departments. Capitalize department names (*Department of Labor, Labor Department*) and titles when they precede a person's name (*Labor Secretary Dahlia Hearst*), but lowercase titles otherwise: *Dahlia Hearst, the labor secretary*. Capitalize the defining department name when standing alone and when necessary for clarity: *New funding for Commerce is actually quite modest,* but avoid overusing that construction, which sounds jargonistic.

cabinet members. See titles of persons.

calf's liver

California (Calif., CA in addresses)

Californian

call-back (noun)

call-down (noun)

call-off (noun)

call-out (noun)

call-over (noun)

calorie(s). Abbreviate, *cal.,* only in maps, charts and tables.

Canada. See individual entries for provinces and territories.

Canal Zone. Abolished by the Panama Canal treaties, which were ratified in 1978. In historical references, abbreviate, *C.Z.,* only in maps, charts and tables. Note that it was *the Canal Zone,* not *the Panama Canal Zone*.

canton. Lowercase except in a name: *the canton of Lucerne (the canton); Canton Lake, Okla.*

canvas/canvass. Canvas is cloth; canvass is to examine or to seek opinions or support.

capital gains, *capital-gains tax*

capitalization. *U.S. News* generally uses a "down" style. For most questions, see separate entries in this book and in the electronic NAMES and PLACES lists. For words not covered here and in those places, consult Webster's New World Dictionary, Third College Edition.

TERMS DERIVED FROM PROPER NOUNS are usually lowercase when used with a specialized meaning: *balkanize, baltimore oriole (bird), brussels sprouts, caesar salad, chinese checkers, ferris wheel, french fries, india ink, manila folder, molotov cocktail, pyrrhic victory, roman numeral, russian roulette, spartan, swiss steak, thespian, yankee pot roast,* but *Scotch whisky* (it's made only in Scotland).

AFTER A COLON. Capitalize the first word only when it begins a complete sentence, when it would normally be capitalized anyway, when it is in a contents-page title or in the rare instance when capitalization is needed for dramatic effect: *He put it this way: The answer is final. They found what they had sought: a final answer. His objective: Victory.* Depending on the effect desired, the initial word following a colon in a headline may be capped even if it does not begin a complete sentence.

PLURALS. When a common noun follows two or more names with which it is combined, lowercase the noun: *the Keystone and Prudential buildings, the Rappahannock and Potomac rivers, Yale and Harvard universities, the State and Interior departments*. But when the noun precedes the capitalized names, it is capitalized: *the Departments of State and Interior, the Universities of Michigan and California, Mounts Monadnock and McKinley.*

SPECIAL EXPRESSION. Capitalizing ordinarily lowercase words to achieve emphasis or irony should generally be avoided in favor of obtaining the same result through sentence structure.

SMALL CAPS, with no quotation marks, may be used for special effect when rendering signs and headlines in body type: *The sign read* DON'T TREAD ON ME. See abbreviations, ages and eras, bylines, central, colon, geographic names, geographic terms, German common nouns, headlines, historic periods, military titles, titles of persons, trademarks, foreign-names entries and other individual entries.

C

captions. STANDARD CAPTIONS are italic, with bold roman lead-ins, and are generally flush left. They usually are full sentences and should then take a period at the end, but they may be less than a full sentence, in which case they take no period:

French connection. *Mideast cafes get some fancy meat choppers.*

French fried. *A little overdone*

TENSE of a caption customarily is the present, even if an event long past is pictured, but avoid absurdities:
Awkward: **Output up.** *Umbrellas leave the factory last July.*
Better: **Output up.** *Umbrellas leaving the factory last July*
MAPS take the following styling:

Italic caps and lowercase
Gulfs
Rivers
Lakes
Oceans
Channels

Full caps, roman
Planets
Countries
States
Provinces

Roman caps and lowercase
Cities
Canals
Railways
Highways

Lightface caps or special styling
Counties

IDENTIFICATION. Make sure to identify all major figures in a photograph, listing them, all other factors being equal, as they appear left to right. Put location words in parentheses:

Berlin break. *Janet Reno (left) greets C. Everett Koop.*

CARTOON CAPTIONS are usually written with quotation marks. If the original caption is already a quote—indicating, for instance, words spoken by a character in the cartoon—our caption still uses only one set of quotation marks. Use a period. Cartoon captions usually are centered, in caps and lowercase: *"A real bad scene."*
See charts and tables, credits, fairness.

cardholder

carry back (verb), *carry-back* (noun and adjective)

carry forward (verb), *carry-forward* (noun and adjective)

carryout (noun and adjective)

carry over (verb), *carry-over* (noun and adjective)

cast-iron ware, but *ironware*

Catholic. Use Roman Catholic, at least on first reference, if that is what is meant. See Roman Catholic Church.

CAT scan. See CT scan.

CB (noun and adjective). Acceptable for citizens' band radio if the meaning is clear.

caucus. Capitalize in a full name; lowercase otherwise: *Congressional Black Caucus, black caucus, the caucus*.

CD-ROM. Abbreviation for compact disc read-only memory. Acceptable on first reference when the meaning is clear.

CDT. See time zones.

Celsius. *150 degrees Celsius, 48°C*. To convert from Fahrenheit, subtract 32, then multiply by five ninths. To convert to Fahrenheit, multiply by 1.8, then add 32.

center on. Don't write "center around." Use *center on* or *cluster around,* etc.

centimeter. Abbreviation, *cm,* acceptable after first reference and in charts and tables. See metric system.

central. Capitalize *central, upper, lower* and *middle* when part of an accepted name; lowercase when merely descriptive: *Central America, Central Europe, central North America, Upper Michigan, Upper Peninsula of Michigan, Lower California* (for Baja California), *Lower East Side* (of Manhattan), *Middle East, upper Midwest*.

Central American (noun and adjective)

century. Lowercase. Spell out under 10: *second century, second century B.C., 16th century, the 1600s, 12th-century building*.
WHEN DOES A CENTURY BEGIN AND END? It's an age-old debate. The 21st century may begin in the year 2001 (the first century was A.D. 1, not A.D. 0), or it may begin in 2000. Some people may wish to wait until the year 2001 to mark the turn of the century, but it can be safely predicted that the few who do will have missed the major celebration. No doubt the big parties will be occurring while the clock strikes midnight Dec. 31, 1999. But writers wishing to avoid an argument might prefer to shun the issue altogether.

chair. *chairman, chairwoman, chairperson*. Capitalize before a name; lowercase otherwise: *Chairman Tessie Van Landingham of the Senate Banking Committee*

(Chairman Van Landingham, the chairman). If you know the titleholder's preference on which word to use, follow it; if not, use *chairman*.

chamber. Capitalize in the name of an organization; lowercase alone: *the Miami Chamber of Commerce (the Chamber of Commerce, the chamber), a chamber of commerce*.

channel. Capitalize with a number: *Channel 3 (the channel)*.

chapter. Capitalize with a number; lowercase alone: *Chapter 11, Chapter IV (the chapter)*.

characters in movies, plays, operas, novels, television shows, etc., are set roman, without quotes: *Henry Fonda played Mr. Roberts in* ***Mr. Roberts***.

charter. Capitalize in a name; lowercase otherwise: *The United Nations Charter (the charter)*.

charts and tables. A typical table:

Rural-crop seesaw

Persimmons soar as sorghum sags

U.S. commodity fluctuations—

	Gain or loss (in tons)	**Change**
Persimmons	460 mil.	+40%
Sorghum	–13 mil.	–12%

Note: Figures are for fiscal 1990. *USN&WR*—Basic data: U.S. Agricuture Dept.

HEADLINE (*Rural-crop seesaw*) may be all caps or caps and lowercase.
CHATTER (*Persimmons soar as sorghum sags*). Capitalize the first word and proper nouns. Use a final period when the chatter is longer than one complete sentence (*Saxophone sales soar. Violins flat.*).
LABEL (*U.S. commodity fluctuations*—) ends with a period if it is a sentence and with a dash, colon, ellipsis points or no punctuation if it is a nonsentence.
COLUMN HEADLINES (*Gain or loss*). Capitalize the first word. Lowercase parenthetical notes (*in tons*).
STUBS (*Persimmons*) and BODY (*460 mil.*). Capitalize the first word and proper nouns.
PLOTTING LABELS (titles characterizing graph lines or bar charts, etc., usually standing nearby in a strategic place) are caps and lowercase.
ABBREVIATIONS, such as *mil.* and *bil.,* are lowercase. *Dept.* is acceptable in credit lines.

PARALLELISM is desirable in line headings. Treat similar items the same: *printers, mechanics and painters,* not *printers, garages and painters*.
KICKERS, notes and credits on charts are not indented. Notes and footnotes end with periods. Credits and source lines do not.
See abbreviations, credits, footnotes, percent, percentage, source lines.

chemicals. Use subscripts in abbreviations: CO_2.

Chicano is acceptable to many Mexican-Americans, but use care when referring to individuals, who may object. See Hispanic.

chief justice. Capitalize before a name; lowercase otherwise: *Chief Justice William Rehnquist (the chief justice)*. Note: The title is *chief justice of the United States,* not *chief justice of the Supreme Court*.

chief of staff. Capitalize before a name; lowercase otherwise: *White House Chief of Staff Mack McLarty, Chief of Staff McLarty, the chief of staff*.

Chinese names. The two primary systems for transliterating Chinese are Pinyin and Wade-Giles. Pinyin is used throughout the mainland and has become the spelling of record in Western academic works and in the Western press. Wade-Giles is still used by many nonmainland Chinese, in Taiwan and in Singapore. Chinese names consist of a family name (almost always one syllable) followed by one or two given names. For subsequent references, only the family name need be used: *Deng Xiaoping (Deng), Li Peng (Li)*. However, if a story refers to several people with the same family name, for example, *Li Peng* and *Li Xiannian,* the whole name should be repeated. In Wade-Giles, given names are hyphenated *(Teng Hsiao-p'ing);* in Pinyin, they are not *(Deng Xiaoping)*. Use Pinyin spellings except for individuals whose preference for another spelling is known, for certain very well known historical figures and for certain well-known place names: *Sun Yat-sen, Chiang Kai-shek* (historical); *Tibet, Mongolia, Taipei* (well-known place names). Some Chinese, especially those who live in or have been educated in the West, have westernized their names, putting the family name last: *Stephen Soo-ming Lo (Lo), James C. H. Shen (Shen)*.
PLACE NAMES: Tiananmen Square, Beijing (not Peking), Guangzhou (not Canton), Chongqing (not Chungking), Nanjing (not Nanking), Yan'an (not Yenan), Shanxi province (not Shansi), Shaanxi province (not Shensi), Jiangsu province (not Kiangsu), Xinjiang autonomous region (not Sinkiang).
DYNASTIES: Qing dynasty (not Ch'ing), Tang dynasty (not T'ang), Zhou dynasty (not Chou). See electronic NAMES and PLACES lists.

chlorofluorocarbons (CFCs)

chord/cord. A chord is a combination of musical notes; a cord is a thin rope, a measure of wood or vocal tissue.

Christmas Eve

church. Capitalize in names of denominations and names of individual churches; lowercase alone: *the Episcopal Church (the church), Grace and Holy Trinity Episcopal Church (the church), an Episcopal church, the Episcopal church next door, Beth El Temple (the temple)*. See denominations and separate entries for particular churches.

Church of Christ, Scientist (Christian Scientists). On subsequent reference, the church. Capstone of the denomination is the Mother Church, named the First Church of Christ, Scientist, in Boston. The Mother Church is run by a five-member board of directors: *Jane Anderson, member of the board of directors (Anderson)*. Local congregations are called branch churches. Their connection is directly with the Mother Church. They operate according to the church manual of the Mother Church, as does the Mother Church itself. Branch churches never use *the* before their names. That is reserved for the Mother Church. A local church would be: *First (Second, Third, etc.) Church of Christ, Scientist (the church)*. Clerical titles are not used by Christian Scientists. A local congregation may have a first reader and a second reader: *Mary Johnson, first reader in Second Church of Christ, Scientist (Johnson)*. Christian Science practitioners work independently of the local churches: *John Barton, a Christian Science practitioner (Barton)*. Lecturers are members of the Board of Lectureship of the Mother Church: *Mavis LaPorte, a Christian Science lecturer (LaPorte)*.

CIA (Central Intelligence Agency) is acceptable on first reference when the meaning is clear.

Circle. Spell out and capitalize in an address; lowercase alone. See addresses.

cities. Whether the name of a city can be used by itself, without an identifying state or country, varies with the article's context and the flow of the news. In general, the cities below do not need to be followed by state or country, but apply common sense in using other names alone or in adding the state or country to any of the cities listed here.

Algiers	Bonn	Copenhagen	Hong Kong
Amsterdam	Boston	Dallas	Honolulu
Anchorage	Brussels	Denver	Houston
Athens	Buenos Aires	Des Moines	Indianapolis
Atlanta	Buffalo	Detroit	Istanbul
Atlantic City	Cairo	Dublin	Jerusalem
Baltimore	Calcutta	Florence	Las Vegas
Beijing	Cape Town	Fort Worth	Leningrad
Beirut	Chicago	Frankfurt	Lisbon
Berlin	Cincinnati	Geneva	London
Bombay	Cleveland	Havana	Los Angeles

Madrid
Manila
Memphis
Mexico City
Miami
Milwaukee
Minneapolis
Montreal
Moscow
Naples
Nashville
New Delhi
New Orleans
New York
Oklahoma City
Omaha
Oslo
Ottawa
Paris
Philadelphia
Phoenix
Pittsburgh
Prague
Quebec
Rio de Janeiro
Rome
St. Louis
Salt Lake City
San Antonio
San Diego
San Francisco
Seattle
Seoul
Shanghai
Stockholm
Tel Aviv
Tokyo
Toronto
Venice
Vienna
Warsaw
Washington
Zurich

citizens' band radio (CB)

city. Capitalize when part of name; lowercase otherwise: *New York City (the city), Atlantic City, Baltimore city* (when necessary to distinguish it, for instance, from the separate *Baltimore County*).

City Council. See council.

civil rights (noun and adjective)

Civil Rights Act of 1991. *the Civil Rights Act, a civil rights act.*

civil service

claim. Do not use as a synonym for *say,* because it indicates that the writer doubts the truth of what is said. A neutral alternative is *assert*.

class. Capitalize with letter or number: *Class II, Class A, Class 12*. Lowercase with a year: *the class of '64*.

club owner

co(-). Write solid except before capitalization or an *o* or in confusing combinations: *co-op, co-author, co-sponsor, co-worker,* but *cooperate, coordinate*.

coach. Capitalize before a name as a title; lowercase otherwise: *Coach Coughlin (the coach)*.

coalfield, but *coal mine, coal miner, coal yard*

coast. Lowercase references to shoreline; capitalize references to a region: *The Pacific coast is dotted with rocky islands; Pacific Coast industries; Pacific Coast states.*

Coast Guard. Capitalize in reference to a particular country's organization: *the U.S. Coast Guard (the Coast Guard),* but *a coast guard, a coast guardsman*.

co-author

C

c.o.d. Acceptable for cash on delivery or collect on delivery when the meaning is clear.

code. Capitalize in an official title; lowercase alone and in a general sense: *Internal Revenue Code (the revenue code, the code), civil code, Federal Criminal Code*.

code-named. Use quotes: *code-named "Popeye."*

coed. As an adjective, *coed* can be a useful alternative to coeducational, but as a noun *student* is usually preferred.

cold-roll (verb)

cold war

colleges and universities. Capitalize college, university, school, academy, institute, etc., when part of a name; lowercase alone: *Harvard University (the university), St. John's College (the college), Pratt Institute (the institute), Sharon Hill High School (the high school in Sharon Hill)*. Capitalize divisions of a college, university, etc., when part of a name; lowercase when expressing a function (departments ordinarily are lowercase on the assumption that the words are functional) and when they are not the official name: *Harvard Law School (Harvard's law school, the law school at Harvard), George Washington University National Law Center* but *George Washington University law school, the Harvard history department, the English department.*
ABBREVIATING NAMES. When you must abbreviate in a chart or a table, do so in this order:
1. Abbreviate *University* as *Univ., College* as *Col., Academy* as *Acad.* and *Institute* as *Inst.*
2. Abbreviate *Technology* as *Tech.*
3. Abbreviate the name of the state (*Univ. of Calif. at Long Beach*).
4. When necessary, if the institution's own preferred shortened name is more understandable to readers than the name determined by these rules (*Penn State* instead of *Pa. State Univ.,* for example), use it. When *Tech* is used as part of a popular name for the school, drop the period (*Georgia Tech*).
Example:
Massachusetts Institute of Technology
Massachusetts Inst. of Technology
Massachusetts Inst. of Tech.
Mass. Inst. of Tech.
When using letter abbreviations, write them solid: *MIT, UCLA, UNC,* but *U.Va.*

CAMPUS NAMES. Distinguish a university's campuses from one another by using *at* and the location, regardless of whether the school itself uses *in,* a comma, a dash, parentheses, a virgule or nothing between the name and the location (*University of Maryland at Baltimore County, University of Maryland at Eastern Shore, State University of New York at Albany, University of California at Los Angeles*). CUNY and SUNY are acceptable in charts and tables for City University of New York and State University of New York, respectively (*CUNY: Hunter College, SUNY College at Fredonia*).
THE. Do not use a capitalized *The* when it appears in front of the name (*American University, College of Idaho, Sage Colleges,* but *College of the Holy Cross, University of the South*). In text, use a lowercase *the* with the name when it sounds natural (*He attends the University of Pennsylvania,* but *She teaches at Pennsylvania State University*).
AND/&. Use *and* except with abbreviations: *Davis and Elkins College, Texas A&M University*.

colloquialisms. See slang, dialect and jargon.

colon. Capitalize the first word that follows a colon when the word: begins a complete sentence; is a proper noun; would otherwise ordinarily be capitalized; needs to be capitalized for dramatic effect, or is in a contents-page title. The first word following a colon in a headline may be capped or not depending on the effect desired. A colon may be used:
TO INTRODUCE QUOTED MATERIAL: *The president said: "I have absolutely no comment."*
TO INTRODUCE A SHORT OR LONG PASSAGE either in or out of quotation marks:
The following article was cabled from Madrid:
The text of Jefferson's address follows:
TO INTRODUCE A SERIES: *The United States faces three pressing problems: unemployment, galloping inflation and spiritual malaise*.
TO SEPARATE THE CLAUSES of a compound sentence when the second clause is an illustration, explanation or restatement of the first: *Jefferson had a drawback: He could not win the golf vote*.
Avoid overusing colons for dramatic effect. In many cases, a comma or semicolon, both of which slow down a reader less than a colon does, will serve just as well. See dash.

colonies. Capitalize in reference to the 13 that became the United States; lowercase otherwise. Lowercase *colonial*.

Coloradan

Colorado (Colo., CO in addresses)

colored. Acceptable, but only in quotes and with an explanation, for references to certain South Africans of racially mixed parentage.

comandante. Spanish military title. Set in italics, but make it roman when it's capped before a name.

combatting, *combatted*

comet. *Halley's comet*. See heavenly bodies.

comma. Commas are used to identify and separate the parts of sentences, clauses and phrases. In some cases, the comma can be omitted without harm. It is sometimes inserted where not needed structurally but where a pause is desired for clarity—which often means the sentence is awkward and should be rewritten.
COORDINATE CLAUSES in a compound sentence are usually separated by a comma: *The premier resigned, and the king fled*. In a short sentence of that type, where clarity is not diminished, the comma can be left out: *The premier resigned and the king fled.* But in a long compound sentence, or a short one where confusion might arise, the comma may be essential. Incorrect: *Jones murdered Smith and Anderson robbed a bank.* (Until the reader readjusts at the word *robbed,* the impression is that Jones murdered Smith and Anderson. A comma is needed.)
SUBORDINATE CLAUSES are usually set off by commas when they appear before the main clause. These commas may sometimes be omitted: *Although commas are useful, they may sometimes be omitted. Although commas are useful they may sometimes be omitted.*
DESCRIPTIVE CLAUSES AND APPOSITIVES are set off with commas: *Senator Blank, who drives a Jaguar, opposes a duty on autos. Her husband, Tom, arrived.* (She has only one husband.)
RESTRICTIVE CLAUSES and appositives are not set off by commas: *The man who said that was undermining foreign policy. Your January 14 article "Whither Dithers?" was terrific.* (There was more than one article January 14.) *Her sister Whitney went home* (when she has more than one sister).
INTRODUCTORY WORDS and phrases are usually set off by commas: *Finally, police used water cannons to drive off the students.* Such a comma can often be omitted without damage: *Yet advisers were perplexed.*
PARENTHETICAL WORDS, phrases or clauses are usually set off by commas: *Subordinate clauses, likewise, are set off.* Or: *Subordinate clauses likewise are set off. A vote of no confidence, he said, would mean ruin.* After *and, but* or *that* at the beginning of a sentence or clause, the comma before the parenthetical matter may be omitted if the sentence remains clear: *And[,] for all I know, she may never return. It is clear that[,] when all is said and done, the fat man has sung.*
ITEMS IN A SERIES are divided by commas. Normally, no comma appears before the final *and: On his farm he grew soybeans, peanuts and corn.* To avoid ambiguity, however, a comma before the final *and* may be needed: *The company's four major divisions were copper, iron and steel, wheat and corn, and cattle.*
WHERE WORDS ARE OMITTED, commas may be substituted: *Mikulski won 42 percent of the vote; Guercio, 23 percent.* Note, however, that if the parts are short and the connection is clear, the commas showing omissions are not mandatory: *Mikulski won 42 percent of the vote, Guercio 23 percent.*

A PERSON'S RESIDENCE OR WORKPLACE is not ordinarily set off by commas:
Tim Connolly of the Budd Co. said . . .
Gov. Rex Denzer of Arkansas said . . .
Senator Allison of Arkansas asked . . .
BEFORE ZIP CODES, no comma is used: *Washington, DC 20037.*
PLUS does not require a preceding comma unless the cadence and structure of the sentence call for it:
Intelligence plus luck pulled him through.
Intelligence, plus a strong element of luck, won out.
OTHER USES of the comma:
On Nov. 18, 1906, he was born.
In April 1977, he shot a bear.
In fourth quarter 1977, he made a profit.
Rockford, Ill.
4,760,200
2400 N Street, N.W., Washington, DC 20037
OVERUSE of commas can be destructive. Since the function of the comma is to break up a sentence into parts whose relationships are clear, insertion of additional commas may confuse the relationships. Incorrect: *When the best farmland is converted to other purposes, agriculture is forced to less productive acreage, and the cost of food production rises.* Everything after the first comma is part of what happens when the best land is converted. The second comma should be omitted. Incorrect: *To ease the strain on pinched borrowers, credit companies, banks and finance houses have stretched out payment schedules.* The first comma sets aside the purpose of the action told in the second part of the sentence. But the commas in the series are piled on, making it seem that pinched borrowers, credit companies, banks, etc., are all parts of the same series. Since the structure of the sentence creates this problem, rewriting is necessary: *Credit companies, banks and finance houses have stretched out payment schedules to ease the strain on pinched borrowers.*
NOT ONLY . . . Do not use a comma in such sentences as *She found that he was not only a liar but also a cheat* unless confusion would otherwise result. **See dash, semicolon.**

commander in chief. Capitalize before a name; lowercase otherwise: *Commander in Chief Mark Schwartz, Commander in Chief Schwartz, the commander in chief.*

commission. Capitalize in a name; lowercase alone: *Federal Communications Commission (the commission), Fulton County Commission (the commission), the Fulton County commissioners.*

committee. Capitalize in names of official groups and in names of organizations; lowercase alone, in names of ad hoc groups, in names of committees of organizations and in plurals: *the House Banking, Finance and Urban Affairs Committee (the Banking Committee, the committee), the Senate committee that deals with postal* *affairs, the Committee for Economic Development, the national committee, the team's membership committee, the finance committee of the Democratic National Committee, the Banking and Foreign Affairs committees.*

C

Commons. Capitalize references to the British House of Commons.

common-stock holder, but *stockholder*

communication refers to the act of communicating.

communications refers to equipment, the industry, etc.

Communion. Capitalize in reference to the Eucharist: *Holy Communion, Communion*. Also, *Lord's Supper.*

communism

Communist. Capitalize when referring to a particular party; lowercase general references: *Communist Party official, the Communist foreign secretary, a Communist, communist ideals*.

compact disc. *CD* is acceptable on second reference when the meaning is clear.

company. Abbreviate and capitalize as part of a name; lowercase alone: *Ford Motor Co. (the company)*. But spell out *company* when it comes at the beginning of a name or when it is plural: *Company B (the company), American Broadcasting Companies. Co.* is not always needed if the reference is clear: *Soundwaves Co. (Soundwaves)*. Use an ampersand, not *and*. See company names.

company names. Abbreviate and capitalize *Co.* and *Corp.,* but spell out *Railroad* and *Railway* as parts of company names when they appear in the body of an article. Abbreviate *Inc.* and *Ltd.* and write without commas. *Inc.* and *Ltd.* are not necessary if *Co., Corp., Railroad, Railway, Sons* or other language clearly indicating a company name is used. But: *Frelinghuysen Chairbottoms Inc., Jesse Filbert Ltd.*

ABBREVIATIONS. *Bro., Bros., R.R.* and *Ry.* may be used in charts, maps and tables. *Co.* and *Corp.* are not always necessary if the name is familiar and the context is clear. *Ford Motor (Ford), General Motors* and *General Electric* are usually acceptable.

AND/AMPERSAND. Use an ampersand in all names of business and legal firms, including savings and loan associations, even when the company prefers *and*. Where the full name of a railroad ends with *Co.,* drop the *Co.* Foreign abbreviations, such as *GmbH, AG, OHG, KG* and *SA,* are usually unnecessary. Where a company's name is to be abbreviated with initials on subsequent reference, omit periods unless they are part of the official name: *Johnson Rotary Pump Co. (JRP), J.R.P. Co. (J.R.P.)*.

ALL-CAPS NAMES. When a company with an all-caps name pronounces the name by its letters, capitalize all the letters (*CSX Corp.*), but when the name is not pronounced by its letters and the letters do not stand for anything, capitalize only the first letter (*Rand Corp.*).
THE. Capitalize *the* only in official or formal contexts: *The Gap* (in a table), *the Gap* (in body type).

compare to, compare with. Use *compare to* when expressing likeness between things usually considered different: *She compared her backhand to a fireball.* Use *compare with* (the far more common usage) when measuring similarities or differences between things usually considered similar: *He compared Jan's backhand with Jill's.*

compass directions. Spell out and lowercase when they indicate mere direction or location: *The balloon headed east; He worked in eastern Virginia; northeastern Nebraska; western Africa.* Capitalize in names; when used alone to designate portions of the world, the continents, nations and states, and when they designate specific, recognized places: *Eastern Hemisphere, East Tennessee, North Korea, West Texas, West Africa, Southern California, South Side* (of Chicago). *The presidential candidates campaigned heavily in the South; Southwest Pacific; West Bank* (of the Jordan); *Middle East; Mideast; Far East; East bloc* (referring to the former Warsaw Pact nations). When in doubt as to whether a designation is specific and recognized, use lowercase. Capitalize adjectives when referring to a region's people or characteristics: *Southern customs, Midwestern farmers, Western allies, Eastern Europe* (in a political rather than a geographic sense). Abbreviate only in maps, charts, tables and addresses: *E., W., S.E., N.N.W.,* etc.

compound sentences. They usually take commas but in some cases need not. See comma.

compound words. In deciding whether to make a compound hyphenated, solid or open, use the following resources:
1. Entries in this book, including the electronic HYPHENS, NAMES and PLACES lists.
2. Webster's New World and Webster's Third International dictionaries.
3. The following guidelines:
NOUNS OF THE MOMENT. Don't run words together unless the dictionary or this book allows it: *bookshop, drugstore,* but *pen shop, doughnut store.*
COMPOUND MODIFIERS. Some compound modifiers (generally made up of an adjective or adverb and a noun) require a hyphen to avoid being misread: *small-animal hospital, strong-defense strategy, toxic-waste dump, primary-care facility;* for other compounds, although a hyphen may not be required for clarity, a hyphen is helpful because its omission could be jarring: *high-stress job.* Some modifiers that are read more easily with a hyphen when used with one noun may not need one when used with a different, familiar construction: *intensive-care study,* but *intensive care unit; liberal-arts orientation,* but *liberal arts degree; mutual-fund admirers,* but *mutual fund salesperson.* If an expression is instantly clear without a

hyphen, drop it: *life insurance policy*. If a combination is in quotation marks, use no hyphens: *a "pay as you play" saxophone,* but if the combination is part of a larger quote, hyphenate it: *He called his music store a "pay-as-you-play emporium."* Combinations that are hyphenated before nouns should not be hyphenated in the predicate—even when they are hyphenated in the dictionary—when the meaning is clear without a hyphen: *He is a part-time employee,* but *he works part time. She is a well-known singer,* but *the singer is well known. She has time-consuming hobbies,* but *her hobbies are time consuming*. If the reader would be confused or impeded by an unhyphenated combination in the predicate, keep the hyphen: *a high-tech piano, the piano was high-tech; a middle-aged bureaucrat, the bureaucrat was middle-aged; open-minded parents, his parents were open-minded*. For compounds that precede the noun, use the following guidelines—
Hyphenate:

- Compounds made up of an adjective and a noun when it might be ambiguous which of the two nouns the adjective modifies: *capital-gains tax, foreign-trade balance, free-trade agreement, frequent-flier bonus, hazardous-waste site, high-court ruling, human-rights abuses, inner-city school, last-minute request, leveraged-buyout firm, low-fat diet, major-medical program, organized-crime group, physical-education class, political-science instructor, primary-care facility, private-property law, public-health policy, public-opinion poll, real-estate broker,* but *affirmative action program, baby boom generation, box office receipts, bulletin board notice, cable television program, civil rights legislation, class action suit, credit card rate, criminal justice system, financial services firm, gun control bill, health care system, heart attack victim, home equity loan, law enforcement agency, liberal arts college, life insurance policy, money market fund, nuclear power plant, property tax rate, trade association newsletter*.
- Compounds with a present participle: *data-processing field, intelligence-gathering equipment, role-playing technique, computer-manufacturing jobs, executive-recruiting firm,* but *ever rising deficits*.
- Compounds with a past participle: *deep-seated anxiety, poverty-stricken family, fine-tuned car, better-educated police,* but *just published book, once debated issue.*
- Compounds made up of an adjective and a noun to which *d* or *ed* has been added: *Democratic-controlled Congress, old-fashioned views, able-bodied worker*.
- Compounds made up of *well* or *ill* and an adjective: *well-worn jeans, ill-gotten gains*.
- Most compounds with a number or ordinal as the first element: *20th-century painting, 7-inch scar, second-grade students, first-quarter profit,* but *10 percent reduction, $100 million aircraft*.
- Most compounds made up of more than two elements: *most-favored-nation status, once-in-a-lifetime opportunity, early-20th-century artist,* but *master of arts degree*. When such constructions become cumbersome (*capital-gains-tax cut*), consider moving the modifier to follow the noun: *a cut in the capital-gains tax*.
- Compounds denoting color: *bluish-green water, blue-green algae, bright-yellow wall, black-and-white photo*. Drop the hyphen after the predicate unless the elements are two colors in the same form: *The water was bluish green. The wall was*

bright yellow. The dress was blue-green.
Do not hyphenate:

- Combinations formed with *very, ever* and *once* and adverbs ending in *ly: very tight jeans, ever tighter circle, once reliable source, carefully chosen words, poorly reasoned argument*. But when the first word is an adjective ending in *ly,* use a hyphen: *scholarly-journal article, hourly-pay issue*.
- Compounds with a letter or numeral as the second element: *Type A behavior, Chapter 11 bankruptcy*.
- Compounds derived from foreign expressions: *ad hoc committee, a priori logic,* but *laissez-faire attitude*.
- Compounds that are chemical terms: *sodium chloride solution*.
- Compounds that are proper nouns: *Dead Sea salt, Third World debate, Pulitzer Prize committee,* but *Pulitzer Prize-winning author*.
- Compounds with a comparative or superlative adjective: *a most thoughtful observer, a less informed source, a more recent photograph*. But exceptions may be made when ambiguity might result without the hyphen: *higher-scoring player, more-hazardous substances, more-affordable houses*. See hyphen.

computer programs, names of. Use italics: ***Excel for Windows, WordPerfect 5.1, Lotus 1-2-3, Release 2.2,*** but set operating systems roman: *Windows, DOS 6*.

conference. Capitalize as part of full official name; lowercase when the accompanying word or words are only a place name or a place name and a date. Do not capitalize when accompanied by descriptive words that do not make up an official title; sometimes mere descriptions are inadvertently raised to official status. Borderline cases will require some judgment: *the Geneva conference of 1954; in 1954, the Geneva conference on Far Eastern affairs; the International Conference on Extermination of Rats (the world conference on rodents, the conference)*.

confirmation. See sacraments.

Congress. Capitalize in reference to U.S. Congress and to the official name of a foreign legislative body. In references such as *Congress of Vienna,* lowercase *congress* by itself.

congressional. Capitalize in the name of a district; lowercase otherwise: *Third Congressional District, 15th Congressional District, the congressional district, a congressional mandate*.

Congressional Black Caucus, but *black caucus, the caucus*

congressman, congresswoman and congressperson are not synonyms for member(s) of the House; senators also are congresspersons. The words can be used for a group of members of Congress, in whichever house, although in practice they most often designate House members. Follow an individual's preference on whether to use congressman, congresswoman or congressperson. See party designation.

Connecticut (Conn., CT in addresses)

Connecticuter

conservative. Capitalize when referring to a political party; lowercase when designating a person's political faith: *the Conservative Party platform, the Conservatives, a conservative point of view.* Since the term often reflects the writer's individual judgment and may not correspond to another writer's interpretation or a reader's, it is best to reserve it for cases on which there is widespread agreement. Where feasible, be more specific: *Senator Shawker, who has usually voted with the opponents of abortion . . . .*

Constitution. Capitalize in a name and alone when referring to a specific national or state constitution: *the U.S. Constitution (the Constitution), the French Constitution (the Constitution), the Arkansas Constitution (the Constitution), a constitution, a constitutional question, a question of constitutionality.*

consul general. Capitalize when used as a title before a name; lowercase otherwise: *Consul General Robert Palmer, the consul general.*

consumer price index. *CPI* is acceptable on second reference.

continent, the. Capitalize when it means Europe: *the Continent,* but *the continent of Europe.*

continental U.S. Don't use for the states below the Canadian border, because Alaska, too, is on the continent. Say *the lower 48, the lower 48 states* or *the 48 contiguous states.*

continual/continuous. Continually means repeatedly; continuously means going on without interruption.

conventions. Capitalize the full name of political conventions: *Democratic National Convention, the national convention, the Republican convention, the convention.*

convict. Do not use with regard to noncriminal proceedings. A person might be *found liable,* for example, in a sex-discrimination case, but the person would not be *convicted* of sex discrimination unless a prison term could be the result. *Found guilty* is similarly problematic in civil cases.

convince, persuade. Convince should never be followed by an infinitive, but persuade may be: *She was convinced that might was right; He was persuaded to give up his gun.*

corporation. Abbreviate and capitalize as part of a name, but spell out when it comes at the beginning; spell out and lowercase alone *(Palisades Corp., the Cor-*

poration for Public Broadcasting, the corporation). Corp. is not always needed if the reference is clear. See company.

corps. Use roman numerals for Army units. Capitalize in a name; lowercase alone: *I Corps (the corps), Transportation Corps (the corps), U.S. Army Corps of Engineers (the Corps of Engineers, the corps)*. See marine.

council. Capitalize in the name of an organization or an agency; lowercase in descriptive uses and when alone: *the Council on Foreign Relations (the council), the Boise City Council (the City Council, the council), executive council of the AFL-CIO, U.N. Security Council (the Security Council, the council)*.

councilor/counselor. A *councilor* is a member of a council; a *counselor* is one who gives advice.

Count. See nobility.

counter( ). Combines solid except before a capitalized word.

countries. Use *it* and *its,* not *she* and *her*.

countries, names of. Spell out where possible, even on maps. For a list of abbreviations that may be used in tight situations, see nations and regions.

county. Capitalize when part of a name; lowercase otherwise: *Sawicki County (the county of Sawicki, the county), the county government, Sawicki and Miller counties*. Irish: *County Cork (the county)*.

couple usually takes a plural verb: *The couple were married in their living room. A couple of songs are enough.* But when it is used to signify a single unit, it takes a singular verb: *Every couple is expected to lead one dance.*

court. Capitalize in an official name as well as in shortened names; lowercase alone or when used descriptively: *the United States Supreme Court (the Supreme Court, the high court, the court), the United States Court of Appeals for the First Circuit (the U.S. Court of Appeals, the First Circuit Court of Appeals, the First Circuit, the Court of Appeals, the appeals court, the court), the Arkansas Supreme Court (the Supreme Court, the court), the Municipal Court of Chicago (the court), the Circuit Court of Montgomery County (the court), Most 17-year-olds when arrested are sent to juvenile court, France's Court of Cassation (the court)*.

court cases. See legal citations.

cover-up (noun and adjective)

crackdown (noun), *crack down* (verb)

credits are all caps. Follow rules for regular copy as to italicizing and use of quotation marks, accents and abbreviations. Positions for credits with photos, cartoons and illustrations are indicated by page layouts. When a credit is not located hard by the work it identifies, include words making clear what the credit relates to: *ILLUSTRATION BY SUSANNE MARIE FOR* ***USN&WR***. When a photographer and an agency are credited together, use a dash (not a hyphen) to link them. This makes the hyphen available for use in a compound name: *WOLFF—BLACK STAR, HENRI CARTIER-BRESSON—MAGNUM, LINDA L. CREIGHTON—****USN&WR***. The names of two agencies given credit for the same photo are separated by a slash: *CONTACT/CAMP*. When one photographer supplies all the photos for a story or for a given page, the style is: *PHOTOS BY CHRISTOPHER SPRINGMANN*. All photos must be credited, including corporate publicity photos, unless specifically noted otherwise by the photo editor. Occasionally, a photographer is credited in the story's byline instead of by using photo credits.
CARTOONS. Note variations in the wording of cartoon credits: *OLIPHANT FOR UNIVERSAL PRESS SYNDICATE, LURIE IN* ***ASAHI SHIMBUN***. Some cartoonists and photographers require the use of a copyright symbol. Cartoons take credits whether or not the signature is legible.
PHOTOS COMMISSIONED BY *USN&WR* are credited as follows: *CHARLIE ARCHAMBAULT FOR* ***USN&WR***. Names of cartoonists, photographers and agencies can be checked with the Photo Department, the electronic CREDITS list or, in many cases, in the Editor & Publisher International Year Book.
COVER CREDITS: *COVER: Photo by Jeff Doda—Sygma*
COVER: Illustration by Doug Johnson Design: WBMG
COMBINATIONS. *ARCHITECT: JAMES BRIDGE; PHOTO: RACHEL WATERS*
MULTIPLE CREDITS. Put the location before the credits:
*PHOTOS (FROM LEFT): BILL AUTH—****USN&WR****; DOUG STONE—AP; AFP.*
See bylines, charts and tables.

criteria. The singular is *criterion;* don't write "a criteria."

cross( ). For spelling, follow the dictionary: *cross section, cross-stitch, crosshatch,* but *crossfire*. Hyphenate made-up combinations.

CST. See time zones.

CT scan. Acceptable for "computered tomography scan" when clear. Also called *CAT* (computerized axial tomography) *scan*. (The American College of Radiology prefers *CT* to *CAT* and *computered* to *computerized*.)

cultural designations. In general, capitalize when referring to a specific style; lowercase in descriptive references: *a Baroque opera,* but *a baroque skateboard*. Follow the dictionary for terms not listed individually in this book.

Cultural Revolution. Capitalize when referring to China's Great Proletarian Cultural Revolution; lowercase otherwise.

currencies. Information about the world's currencies is kept up to date by three periodicals: *International Financial Statistics,* published monthly by the International Monetary Fund; *Monthly Bulletin of Statistics,* published by the United Nations, and *Statistical Release H-10,* which is issued weekly by the Federal Reserve Board.

Country or region	**Basic unit**	**Chief fractional unit**
Afghanistan	afghani	pul(s)
Albania	lek(e)	qintar(s)
Algeria	dinar(s)	centime(s)
American Samoa	dollar(s)	cent(s)
Andorra	French franc(s) and Spanish peseta(s)	centime(s) centimo(s)
Angola	kwanza(s)	lwei(s)
Anguilla	dollar(s)	cent(s)
Antigua & Barbuda	dollar(s)	cent(s)
Argentina	peso(s)	centavo(s)
Armenia	ruble(s)	kopeck(s)
Aruba	guilder(s)	cent(s)
Australia	dollar(s)	cent(s)
Austria	schilling(s)	groschen
Azerbaijan	manat*	gapik*
Bahamas	dollar(s)	cent(s)
Bahrain	dinar(s)	fils
Bangladesh	taka(s)	paisa (paise)
Barbados	dollar(s)	cent(s)
Belarus	ruble(s)*	kopeck(s)*
Belgium	franc(s)	centime(s)
Belize	dollar(s)	cent(s)
Benin	franc(s)	centime(s)
Bermuda	dollar(s)	cent(s)
Bhutan	ngultrum(s)	chetrum(s)
Bolivia	peso(s)	centavo(s)
Botswana	pula	thebe
Brazil	cruzeiro(s)	centavo(s)
Brunei	dollar(s)	cent(s)
Bulgaria	lev(a)	stotinka (stotinki)
Burkina Faso	CFA franc(s)	centime(s)
Burundi	franc(s)	centime(s)
Cambodia	riel(s)	sen
Cameroon	CFA franc(s)	centime(s)
Canada	dollar(s)	cent(s)
Cape Verde	escudo(s)	centavo(s)
Cayman Islands	dollar(s)	cent(s)
Central African Republic	CFA franc(s)	centime(s)
Chad	CFA franc(s)	centime(s)

Country or region	Basic unit	Chief fractional unit
Chile	peso(s)	centesimo(s)
China	yuan	fen
Colombia	peso(s)	centavo(s)
Comoros	franc(s)	centime(s)
Congo	CFA franc(s)	centime(s)
Costa Rica	colon(s)	centimo(s)
Croatia	dinar(s)	(none)
Cuba	peso(s)	centavo(s)
Cyprus	pound(s)	cent(s)
Czech Republic	crown(s)	haler(s)
Denmark	krone(r)	ore
Djibouti	franc(s)	centime(s)
Dominica	dollar(s)	cent(s)
Dominican Republic	peso(s)	centavo(s)
Ecuador	sucre(s)	centavo(s)
Egypt	pound(s)	piaster
El Salvador	colon(s)	centavo(s)
Equatorial Guinea	ekuele(s)	centimo(s)
Eritrea	birr	cent(s)
Estonia	kroon(s)	sent(s)
Ethiopia	birr	cent(s)
Falkland Islands	pound(s)	penny (pence)
Fiji	dollar(s)	cent(s)
Finland	markka(a)	penni (pennia)
France	franc(s)	centime(s)
Gabon	CFA franc(s)	centime(s)
Gambia	dalasi	butut
Georgia	ruble(s)*	kopeck(s)*
Germany	deutsche mark(s)	pfennig(s)
Ghana	cedi(s)	pesewa(s)
Great Britain	pound(s)	penny (pence)
Greece	drachma(s)	lepton (lepta)
Grenada	dollar(s)	cent(s)
Guatemala	quetzal(es)	centavo(s)
Guinea	franc(s)	centime(s)
Guinea-Bissau	peso(s)	centavo(s)
Guyana	dollar(s)	cent(s)
Haiti	gourde(s)	centime(s)
Honduras	lempira(s)	centavo(s)
Hong Kong	Hong Kong dollar(s)	cent(s)
Hungary	forint(s)	filler
Iceland	krona (kronur)	eyrir (aurar)
India	rupee(s)	paisa (paise)
Indonesia	rupiah(s)	sen
Iran	rial(s)	dinar(s)

Country or region	**Basic unit**	**Chief fractional unit**
Iraq	dinar(s)	fils
Ireland	pound(s)	penny (pence)
Isle of Man	pound(s)	penny (pence)
Israel	shekel(s)	agora (agorot)
Italy	lira (lire)	centesimo(s)
Ivory Coast	CFA franc(s)	centime(s)
Jamaica	dollar(s)	cent(s)
Japan	yen	sen
Jordan	dinar(s)	fils
Kazakhstan	ruble(s)*	kopeck(s)*
Kenya	shilling(s)	cent(s)
Kirgizstan	som(s)	tyiyn(s)
Kiribati	Australian dollar(s)	cent(s)
Kuwait	dinar(s)	fils
Laos	kip(s)	at
Latvia	lats (lati)	santims (santimi)
Lebanon	pound(s)	piaster
Lesotho	loti (maloti)	lisente
Liberia	dollar(s)	cent(s)
Libya	dinar(s)	dirham
Liechtenstein	Swiss franc(s)	centime(s)
Lithuania	litas (litai)	centas (centai)
Luxembourg	franc(s)	centime(s)
Macao	pataca(s)	avo(s)
Macedonia	denar(s)	(none)
Madagascar	franc(s)	centime(s)
Malawi	kwacha	tambala (matambala)
Malaysia	ringgit(s)	sen
Maldives	rufiyaa	lari
Mali	franc(s)	centime(s)
Malta	lira	cent(s)
Mauritania	ouguiya(s)	khoums
Mauritius	rupee(s)	cent(s)
Mexico	peso(s)	centavo(s)
Moldova	ruble(s)*	kopeck(s)*
Monaco	French franc(s)	centime(s)
Mongolia	tugrik(s)	mongo(s)
Morocco	dirham(s)	centime(s)
Mozambique	metical (meticais)	centavo(s)
Myanmar	kyat(s)	pya(s)
Namibia	rand	(none)
Nauru	Australian dollar(s)	cent(s)
Nepal	rupee(s)	pice
Netherlands	guilder(s)	cent(s)
New Zealand	dollar(s)	cent(s)

Country or region	**Basic unit**	**Chief fractional unit**
Nicaragua	cordoba(s)	centavo(s)
Niger	CFA franc(s)	centime(s)
Nigeria	naira	kobo
North Korea	won	jeon
Norway	krone(r)	ore
Oman	rial(s)	baiza(s)
Pakistan	rupee(s)	paisa (paise)
Panama	balboa(s)	cent(s)
Papua New Guinea	kina	toea
Paraguay	guaraní(s)	centimo(s)
Peru	sol(s)	inti(s)
Philippines	peso(s)	centavo(s)
Poland	zloty(s)	grosz(y)
Portugal	escudo(s)	centavo(s)
Puerto Rico	dollar(s)	cent(s)
Qatar	riyal(s)	dirham
Réunion	franc(s)	centime(s)
Romania	leu (lei)	ban(i)
Russia	ruble(s)	kopeck(s)
Rwanda	franc(s)	centime(s)
St. Christopher and Nevis	dollar(s)	cent(s)
St. Lucia	dollar(s)	cent(s)
San Marino	Italian lira	centesimo(s)
São Tomé and Príncipe	dobra(s)	centavo(s)
Saudi Arabia	riyal(s)	halala
Scotland	pound(s)	penny (pence)
Senegal	CFA franc(s)	centime(s)
Seychelles	rupee(s)	cent(s)
Sierra Leone	leone(s)	cent(s)
Singapore	dollar(s)	cent(s)
Slovakia	koruna (koruny)	haler (haleru)
Slovenia	tolar(s)	stotin(s)
Solomon Islands	dollar(s)	cent(s)
Somalia	shilling(s)	cent(s)
South Africa	rand	cent(s)
South Korea	won	chon
Soviet Union	ruble(s)	kopeck
Spain	peseta(s)	centimo(s)
Sri Lanka	rupee(s)	cent(s)
Sudan	pound(s)	piaster
Suriname	guilder(s)	cent(s)
Swaziland	lilangeni (emalangeni)	cent(s)
Sweden	krona (kronor)	centime(s)
Switzerland	franc(s)	centime(s)
Syria	pound(s)	piaster

Country or region	**Basic unit**	**Chief fractional unit**
Taiwan	dollar(s)	cent(s)
Tajikistan	ruble(s)*	kopeck(s)*
Tanzania	shilling(s)	cent(s)
Thailand	baht(s)	satang
Togo	CFA franc(s)	centime(s)
Tonga	pa'anga	seniti
Transkei	rand	cent(s)
Trinidad and Tobago	dollar(s)	cent(s)
Tunisia	dinar(s)	millime
Turkey	lira(s)	kurus
Turkmenistan	ruble(s)*	kopeck(s)*
Tuvalu	Australian dollar(s)	cent(s)
Uganda	shilling(s)	cent(s)
Ukraine	karbovanets(i)*	(none)*
United Arab Emirates	dirham(s)	fils
Uruguay	peso(s)	centesimo(s)
Uzbekistan	ruble(s)	kopeck(s)
Vanuatu	vatu	(none)
Venezuela	bolívar(es)	centimo(s)
Vietnam	dong	xu
Virgin Islands	dollar(s)	cent(s)
Wales	pound(s)	penny (pence)
Western Samoa	tala	sene
Yemen	riyal(s)	fils
Yugoslavia	dinar(s)	para
Zaire	zaire(s)	likuta (makuta)
Zambia	kwacha(s)	ngwee
Zimbabwe	dollar(s)	cent(s)

* Names for currencies of some former republics of the Soviet Union are in flux. Check with the nation's embassy or U.N. delegation for the latest information.

cut back (verb), *cutback* (noun and adjective)

cut off (verb), *cutoff* (noun and adjective)

Czech, Czechoslovak. The Czech and Slovak languages are closely related but distinct from each other. Use *Czech* when referring to the Czech language and the Czech Republic and to Czech culture before the existence of the Republic of Czechoslovakia (1918-92): *The address was broadcast in Czech. She joined the Czech Army in 1993. The Czech composer Smetana relied heavily on folk tunes.* Use *Slovak* similarly. Use *Czechoslovak* for overall references to the people or government of what was Czechoslovakia: *The Czechoslovak capital was Prague. Soviet forces arrested 1,500 Czechoslovak citizens.*

D

'Style should be the servant of clarity and understanding—supportive, but unobtrusive, so that the reader doesn't really know it's there.'

SUSAN DENTZER
SENIOR ECONOMIC
CORRESPONDENT

da. See particles.

Dalai Lama. Capitalize when referring to an individual: *The Dalai Lama returned from exile.* Lowercase otherwise: *Who will be the next dalai lama?*

dam. Capitalize when part of a name; lowercase otherwise: *Grand Coulee Dam (the dam)*.

dash. Dashes are used as substitutes for commas, parentheses, colons and brackets. They are more spectacular than commas and therefore more arresting, but compared with parentheses and brackets they cause less interruption in the flow of copy. As punctuation to introduce a collection of material, they appear more sweeping and less specific than colons. Use an em dash (shift hyphen) in body type, subheads, captions and precedes; use an en dash (supershift hyphen), shorter than an em dash but longer than a hyphen, in headlines and decks.
Use the dash to:
SET OFF A PARENTHETICAL EXPRESSION: *The race is on—Pride was the favorite—and the winner loses all.*
INTRODUCE A SERIES: *This year's race includes three Southern candidates—McCool, Wills and Handley.*
INTRODUCE A SECTION or an entire article. It is especially useful to substitute a dash for a colon if the section to follow will itself have sentences or subsections introduced by colons:

Here are reactions around the country—A pipefitter in Sioux City: "I think . . ."
OBTAIN EMPHASIS before a final word, phrase or clause: *One thing he wanted more than any other—to be president. He wanted to win the presidency—and he won it.*
TERMINATE AN INTERRUPTED QUOTATION:
Q. What is your greatest ambition, Senator?
A. As to what I want—
Q. I mean politically, not personally.
But a quote that just trails off should end with an ellipsis: *"I might run," Matthews said, "if . . . ."*
CAUTION. Since the dash is more impressive typographically than the comma and a more commanding stop, overuse of dashes is even worse than overuse of commas. One dash or pair of dashes is enough for a paragraph, and use in successive paragraphs is often too much. Too many dashes in a single sentence can lead to confusion:
Herbert—the Republican candidate—if she wins in Nebraska—will be a cinch to go all the way. The dashes read like a pair, but they are not.
AN EN DASH may be substituted for a hyphen in some cases, for clarity: *Popular Front for the Liberation of Palestine–General Command (PFLP–GC), American Federation of Labor–Congress of Industrial Organizations, white-collar–blue-collar contrast, New York–great-circle route, Minneapolis–St. Paul.* See hyphen.

data is plural. Write *these data,* not *this data.*

datelines. When used at the beginning of an article, capitalize: *SIERRA VISTA, ARIZ.* When used in a byline, follow the style of the byline. See cities.

dates. *Dec. 15, 1955; December 15; December 1955; 1950s; 1906-85,* but spell out the month on the cover and in the running foot regardless of length: *December 15, 1993.*

day. Capitalize the names of holidays or special days: *Election Day, Mother's Day, Inauguration Day, Veterans Day.*

Day 1, *Day 13,* but *the 13th day*

de. See French names, particles.

de( ). Generally combines solid except before a capitalized letter or an *e: de-Stalinization, de-emphasize.*

deacon. See entries under individual churches.

death knell

death row

Dec. See dates, months.

decades. In general, use figures, but spell out when appropriate to the context: *'50s, 1950s, lost in the Fifties, 1920s, '20s, Roaring Twenties, mid-'60s.*

decimals. Use figures. For amounts less than 1, use a 0 before the decimal point if confusion could otherwise result.

D

Deepfreeze. The trademark of a brand of food freezer is one word, capitalized: *They sold only the Deepfreeze brand.* Other uses are lowercase, two words or hyphenated: *He gave her the deep freeze. She issued a deep-freeze warning.*

Deep South. See political regions.

degrees. See temperature.

degrees, academic. See bachelor of arts degree, juris doctor, etc.

deity. Capitalize names of the Supreme Being, names of lesser gods and appellations meaning God: *Allah, God, Jehovah, Yahweh, Holy Ghost, the Almighty, the Father, the King of Kings, the Lamb of God, the Prince of Peace, Apollo, Zeus.* Lowercase pronouns *he, him,* etc.

Delaware (Del., DE in addresses)

Delawarean

delegate at large (noun), *delegate-at-large* (adjective)

deletions. See ellipsis points, quotations.

demi( ). Write solid except before a capitalization or an *i*.

Democratic National Committee (*the national committee, the committee, Democratic State Committee*)

Democratic National Convention (*the national convention, the party convention, the convention*)

Democratic Party. *Democrats, the party*. Abbreviation, *Dem.* or *D,* is acceptable only in maps, charts, tables and parenthetical identifications: *Karen Kraft (D-Minn.),* but for ways to avoid using parenthetical IDs see party designation.

denominations, church. Following are names of some representative denominations from the list of more than 200 published by the National Council of the Churches of Christ in the U.S.A.:

African Methodist Episcopal Church
African Methodist Episcopal Zion Church
American Baptist Churches in the U.S.A.
Assemblies of God
Christian Church (Disciples of Christ)
Christian Churches and Churches of Christ
Church of Christ, Scientist
Church of Jesus Christ of Latter-day Saints (Mormons)
Episcopal Church
Evangelical Friends Alliance
Evangelical Lutheran Church in America
Friends General Conference
Friends United Meeting
Greek Orthodox Archdiocese of North and South America
Hungarian Reformed Church in America
Jehovah's Witnesses
Lutheran Church—Missouri Synod
Moravian Church in America
National Baptist Convention of America
National Baptist Convention, U.S.A. Inc.
Orthodox Church in America (formerly Russian Orthodox Greek Catholic Church of America)
Pentecostal Assemblies of the World Inc.
Pentecostal Holiness Church, International
Polish National Catholic Church of America
Presbyterian Church (U.S.A.)
Religious Society of Friends (Conservative)
Religious Society of Friends (Unaffiliated Meetings)
Reorganized Church of Jesus Christ of Latter Day Saints
Roman Catholic Church
Romanian Orthodox Episcopate of America
Serbian Orthodox Church in the U.S.A. and Canada
Seventh-Day Adventist Church
Southern Baptist Convention
Syrian Orthodox Church of Antioch
Ukrainian Orthodox Church in America
Union of American Hebrew Congregations (Reform)
Union of Orthodox Jewish Congregations of America (Orthodox)
Unitarian Universalist Association
United Church of Christ (includes the former Evangelical and Reformed Church and most former Congregational Christian churches. Structure and terminology vary; check locally)
United Methodist Church
United Synagogue of Conservative Judaism (Conservative)

HELP WITH QUESTIONS. A valuable source for names of denominations, church statistics and histories, headquarters addresses and telephone numbers is the

Yearbook of American and Canadian Churches, which is published by the National Council of Churches, 475 Riverside Drive, New York, NY 10115. The telephone number for the yearbook is (800) 672-1789. The telephone number of the council's public relations office is (212) 870-2227. See entries under individual church names.

department. Capitalize in the name of a primary agency of government and when part of the name of a company; lowercase alone and when part of the name of a subdivision of an agency or company: *Department of Justice (Justice Department, the department), the Departments of State and Agriculture,* but *the State and Agriculture departments, Rodney's Department Store, the clothing department*. Capitalize the names of other nations' comparable agencies: *Foreign Ministry (the ministry)*. Lowercase departments of schools and colleges: *the Swarthmore history department, the English department*. Abbreviation, *Dept.,* is permitted in chart and table credits.

Depression, the. Capitalize in references to the period that began in 1929; lowercase otherwise. Also *Great Depression*.

des. See particles.

desalination means the same as desalinization, so use the shorter word.

descriptive clauses. See that, which.

(-)designate. Hyphenate: *President-designate Jim Son, the president-designate*.

deutsche mark(s). German currency, commonly called *mark*.

devil. Capitalize when it means Satan; lowercase otherwise: *The Devil made me do it. A devil made me do it. They say devils live there.*

diacritics. See accent marks.

dialect. See accents; slang, dialect and jargon.

dice is plural; the singular is *die*.

dictionaries. Write names of dictionaries roman, no quotes. *U.S. News* uses:
1. Webster's New World Dictionary, Third College Edition (Simon & Schuster, 1988). It is the first choice for spelling and definitions not included in this book.
2. Webster's Third International Dictionary (Merriam-Webster, 1981). Use this as a backup for spelling, but for word usage it is not as reliable as the New World.
3. Webster's New Geographical Dictionary (Merriam-Webster, 1988), backup source for place names. See geographic names, spelling.

die-cast (adjective), *die casting* (noun)

digital audiotape. *DAT* acceptable on second reference when the meaning is clear.

disabled. Used as an adjective, this is preferred to "handicapped": *disabled man, disabled person, disabled people, disabled veteran*. Avoid using the word as a noun (*the disabled*), which emphasizes disability at the expense of individuality. See victim.

disburse/disperse. Disburse is to pay out; disperse is to scatter.

disc. In general, use *disk,* but use *disc* for phonograph records and compact discs, and see below and follow the dictionary for certain other exceptions. Follow the company's spelling on trademarked names: *Sony's Mini Disc*.

disc brake

disc harrow

disc jockey

diseases. In general, write them lowercase, except for any proper names they may contain: *measles, osteoarthritis, emphysema, atherosclerosis, Parkinson's disease, Hodgkin's disease*. Recommended references: Stedman's Medical Dictionary, Dorland's Illustrated Medical Dictionary, AMA Encyclopedia of Medicine, AMA Family Medical Guide, The Merck Manual.

disk is the standard spelling, but follow certain exceptions listed above and in the dictionary.

diskette, *computer disk, disk drive, hard disk, floppy disk*

disk wheel

disperse. See disburse/disperse.

dissociate means the same as *disassociate,* so use the shorter word.

district. Capitalize in names of congressional and legislative districts; lowercase alone except in reference to the District of Columbia: *23rd Congressional District (23rd District, the district)*.

District of Columbia (D.C., DC in addresses), *the District*

District of Columbia resident(s), *District resident, D.C. resident, Washingtonian*

divebomb (verb), *dive bomber* (noun)

division. Capitalize when used with a specific military number or designation; lowercase alone: *45th Division (the division), 2nd Airborne Division (the division).* Lowercase when in the name of a subdivision of an agency or a company: *antitrust division of the Justice Department, Chevrolet division of General Motors.*

D

DMZ. Acceptable on second reference to demilitarized zone.

do. See particles.

doctor (Dr., Drs.). Abbreviate when used as a title before a name; spell out otherwise. Use *Dr.* as a title with a person's name only in quoted matter or when needed for clarity, as when husbands and wives need to be distinguished from each other, and use only when the degree is earned (not honorary). If *Dr.* is used, specify the type of doctorate the person holds, keeping in mind that most readers presume that *Dr.* refers to a medical doctor.

doctor of dental surgery (D.D.S.), *a doctor of dental surgery degree*

doctor of divinity (D.D.)

doctor of laws. See juris doctor.

doctor of medicine (M.D.)

doctor of philosophy (Ph.D.)

doctrine. Capitalize in a recognized name; lowercase alone: *Monroe Doctrine (the doctrine), Brezhnev Doctrine, preaching an isolationist doctrine.*

dollar(s). Abbreviate, *dol.,* only in maps, tables and charts. Use the dollar sign with figures: *$3 million.*

do's and don'ts

double genitive. In possessive expressions that use *of* and *'s,* the *'s,* although idiomatic, can often be used or dropped with no ill effect (*a friend of the girl's, a friend of the girl*), but in some cases the 's is required for understanding:
an opinion of the tutor's (an opinion held by the tutor)
an opinion of the tutor (someone else's opinion of the tutor)
a portrait of Chagall's (the portrait was created by Chagall)
a portrait of Chagall (Chagall is the subject of the portrait)
In some cases, a different preposition might work better: *a portrait by Chagall.* With pronouns, idiom invariably calls for the possessive form: *a friend of mine, a book of yours.*

double modifiers. See compound words.

Dow Jones. *Dow Jones industrial average (the Dow average)*. The number takes no comma: *3446.68*.

download

down payment

downriver

Down's syndrome. But note that some organizations drop the apostrophe and s in their names (National Down Syndrome Congress).

downtrend

down under (Australia or New Zealand, but *down-under policies*)

Dr. See doctor.

drop in (verb), *drop-in* (noun)

drop off (verb), *drop-off* (noun)

drop out (verb), *dropout* (noun)

drugs. They include prescription and nonprescription pharmaceutical products, illicit substances such as heroin and marijuana as well as beverage alcohol and tobacco products, so take care to use precise terms. For instance, don't write *He was addicted to drugs and alcohol* because alcohol is a drug and *drugs* is imprecise. Better: *He was addicted to alcohol and barbiturates.*
NAMES. In most cases, pharmaceutical drugs should be referred to by their generic names rather than by brand names: *sulfisoxazole,* not *Gantrisin; tetracycline hydrochloride,* not *Achromycin.* But if a point is being made about a particular brand, the brand name should be used. In some contexts, it may be desirable to use both names, as: *Gantrisin, a brand of sulfisoxazole*. Brands generally are capitalized, generic names lowercased.
REFERENCES. Good sources for information are the Physicians' Desk Reference and *Drug Information for the Consumer,* published by *Consumer Reports* and the U.S. Pharmacopeial Convention.

drunk. *drunken driver, drunken driving,* but *He was drunk.*

dry goods (noun), *dry-goods store* (adjective)

du. See particles, Du Pont.

due. Correct when *due* modifies a noun: *rain due to a cold front* or *autos due this fall*. Incorrect when there is no modified noun, as in *She went due to an emergency*. In that case, use *because of* instead.

duke. See nobility.

Du Pont. This name takes various forms in different branches of the family. The company's full name is *E. I. du Pont de Nemours & Co.,* but it's *the DuPont Co.* or *DuPont* (no space between *Du* and *Pont*). See the electronic NAMES list.

duty-free. *She mailed the duty-free gifts. These goods moved duty free.*

E

'There are only two stories on the financial markets. Up and down. And down and up.'

JACK EGAN
ASSISTANT MANAGING EDITOR

earl. See nobility.

earth. Lowercase except when personified or when referring to the planet: *rich, dark earth; down to earth; returning to Earth; Can the Earth survive?; "I am the daughter of Earth and Water"; traveling from Mars to Earth; traveling from Earth to the moon; They built the largest telescope on Earth.*

east, eastern. See compass directions.

East Room (of the White House)

easy money (noun), *easy-money* (adjective)

ecology is a branch of biology. Do not use it as a synonym for *ecosystem* or *environment*.

Economic Report. Capitalize references to the president's annual report: *Economic Report of the President, President Bush's Economic Report (his Economic Report, the report)*.

ECU (ECUs). Acceptable on second reference to European currency unit(s).

editors' notes. See bylines.

EDT. See time zones.

effect. See affect/effect.

(-)elect. *President-elect Lauch (the president-elect)*.

Election Day

Electoral College

electric, electronic, electronics. Electric light bulbs and electric motors are run by electricity. Electronic pianos and electronic rectifiers are operated by a flow of electrons controlled by tubes or transistors. Electronics is a branch of physics: *electronics industry*.

ellipsis points. Use an ellipsis (three points, separated by thin spaces so they won't be broken over a line) to indicate deletions in quotes, textual matter and documents. Put a regular space before and after the ellipsis *(The law states: "He shall be hanged . . . till dead.")*. Use a period and three points when the deletion occurs after the end of a sentence *("That was the end of the case. . . . Sentencing came on Tuesday.")*. If you break off a sentence before the end, put a space before the period, then an ellipsis *("That was the end . . . . Sentencing came on Tuesday.")*. Retain the original punctuation before or after a deletion only if necessary to the sense of the sentence:
"To sharpen the knife, you must use a stone."
"To sharpen the knife . . . use a stone."
"Observe these herbs: thyme, rosemary and oregano."
"Observe these herbs: . . . rosemary and oregano."

E-mail. Acceptable on second reference to electronic mail.

embassy. Capitalize in a name; lowercase alone: *the Canadian Embassy (the embassy), the French and Canadian embassies*.

emigrate. People emigrate *from* and immigrate *to: She emigrated from France. He immigrated to the United States.*

employee

encyclopedias. Set names roman, no quotes. See book titles.

en dash. Longer than a hyphen, shorter than the standard dash (em dash), it is used in place of a dash in headlines. In body type, it may be substituted for a hyphen to promote clarity: *white-collar–blue-collar contrast*. To get an en dash, hit supershift hyphen. See dash.

engine. Generally, use *engine* for devices that develop their own power, *motor* for devices powered by external means: *airplane engine, electric motor, a car engine's starter motor.*

-engine. *four-engine plane.*

en route

ensure. To make sure or make safe. Use *insure* with regard to insurance. Use *assure* when the meaning is "to convince" or "to promise confidently."

E

Episcopal Church. On subsequent reference, *the church*. Members are *Episcopalians*. The adjective is *Episcopal. The Rev. Andrew Tucker, deacon of St. Dunstan's Episcopal Church (the deacon)*. Some priests prefer to be addressed as *Father* or *Mother. The Rev. Janice Parker, rector of All Souls' Episcopal Church (Mother Parker, Parker, the minister, a minister); Suffragan Bishop Donald Schurick of Virginia,* or *of the Diocese of Virginia (Bishop Schurick, the bishop); Canon Elise Andrews (Canon Andrews, the canon). Presiding Bishop James Grier of the Episcopal Church (Presiding Bishop Grier, Bishop Grier, the presiding bishop, the bishop); the Very Rev. Catherine Stevens, dean of Birmingham Cathedral (Dean Stevens, the dean).*

epithets. Do not use derogatory terms for racial, national, religious, sectional or ethnic groups or demeaning language related to color, creed, sex, age, marital status, national origin, personal appearance, political affiliation or mental or physical disability, except in quotations and then only when absolutely essential to a story. See fairness, gender bias.

eras. See ages and eras.

EST. See time zones.

establishment. Lowercase, it often appears with a modifier, *the recording-industry establishment,* and refers to an organization or a grouping of tangentially related interests. Capitalized, as in *the Establishment,* it should be used sparingly and by itself to refer to an inner group that holds controlling power.

ethnic identification. Do not use unless it is clearly relevant to a story.

Eucharist. See sacraments.

Euro( ). Hyphenate when followed by capitalization; otherwise make solid: *Euro-Communist, Eurodollar.*

European Communities (EC). See electronic NAMES list.

even money (noun), *even-money* (adjective)

ever. Do not hyphenate in constructions like *ever increasing income.*

every day (adverb): *He goes every day; everyday* (adjective): *an everyday trip.*

ex. Write solid except in Latin phrases and when it means former: *ex officio, ex-writer.*

exact words. Define your terms. What is "upper class"? What is "middle class"? Is the next class down "lower class"? Do you mean "middle income"? What is "Northeast"? In the search for exact terms, it's helpful to avoid, when possible, words that are used imprecisely:
At Columbus, Ohio, a new ***facility*** *for the Nessel Co. is nearing completion.* What is it? A bathroom? A 3-acre factory?
In Denver, a new library is ***underway.*** Is somebody campaigning for a new library? Are plans being drawn for one? Has ground been broken for it? Is work nearly complete on it? Is the library already in operation? Is the library going somewhere?
Many *villages have closed their local jails.* Hundreds? More than 100? Dozens? Ten?

excess-profits tax

exclamation mark. Use very sparingly. It goes inside quotation marks when part of a quotation, outside otherwise.

execute, execution. These involve legal killing. Do not use for, say, a gangland or guerrilla slaying. In those cases, use such expressions as *execution-style killing.*

Executive Office (of the president of the United States)

executive order. Capitalize when part of a name; lowercase otherwise: *The president issued Executive Order 107. The president issued an executive order.*

exhibit. Capitalize with a letter or a number: *Exhibit A, Exhibit 13 (the exhibit).*

expert. Avoid overuse or misuse. Not everyone who pontificates on an issue is an expert. *Specialist* is often a more objective alternative.

Export-Import Bank. Abbreviation, *Ex-Im Bank,* acceptable on second reference.

extra( ). Meaning outside or beyond, it usually combines solid except before a capitalization or an *a: extramarital, extraordinary,* but *extra-base hit*. Meaning "especially," it is hyphenated: *extra-expensive.*

eye to eye. *They saw eye to eye, an eye-to-eye confrontation*. Use *eyeball* similarly.

F

'Every voice should have the opportunity to be heard, however insignificant it might appear to be.'

MYKE FREEMAN
CHIEF NEWS ASSISTANT

facade

face lift

face to face. *They stood face to face, a face-to-face standoff.*

fact finder

fact-finding (noun and adjective)

fairness. A good general approach is to apply the golden rule: Imagine yourself as the object of any characterizations or aspersions in your story and treat the individuals involved as you would wish to be treated yourself. Extreme care is required in dealing with criminal charges, lawsuits and other accusations and personal matters, such as sexual behavior and situations involving children.
FACTUAL CORRECTNESS is the first, though indeed not the only, consideration. Newspaper clippings and wire-service items are not enough backup when crime or misbehavior is concerned. We have to get as close as possible to sources on the public record. Quoting a person or publication does not excuse us for a mistake of fact or judgment, even though in some cases we can show better faith by attributing a statement than by making it on our own.
UP-TO-DATE INFORMATION is essential. It is unsafe to write without checking the possibility of appeal, new evidence or other change. Therefore, we must keep

current, never working just from old material.
BOTH SIDES are important. If a person is accused in any manner or the person's position is attacked, every effort must be made to present the individual's reply. If our sources have not provided any response, it is up to us to look for one. If a reference by a person being interviewed may be harmful to another person, efforts should be made to contact the other person.
SUITABLE WORDS are a matter for careful choice and examination, to avoid any implication of guilt when guilt has not been proved in court. "Arrested *for* theft," for example, may be read as implying guilt. "Arrested *on a charge of* theft" is one right way to say it if that really is the charge—and we must make certain it is an official charge. *The culprits* and similar phrases make trouble on two counts. First, they lump together several individuals, some of whom may suffer by association. Second, they may indicate guilt when no guilt has been proved.
ALLEGATIONS of bad behavior by a public official may be actionable unless they concern the administration of office. Doubt has been cast on the defense that social prominence opens the way to damaging news. And the excuse that a mistake was made without malice may be turned down by courts.
CAPTION WRITING presents a special risk. Crowd scenes in which people can be identified are often troublesome. For instance, if a photograph illustrates a crime or disorder, our description must be tailored to avoid implicating any persons who might be innocent bystanders. A child's face in a story about classes for the retarded must be treated with the utmost caution: If the child is not retarded, we could get into serious trouble by leaving any implication that the child might be; but even if the child is, we might have to worry about causing pain or embarrassment. The photographer is responsible for getting releases signed for photographs, and the photo editor is responsible for making sure the photo has a release before it is published, but we must ensure that captions and contexts do not go beyond the purposes understood by the signers.
LEGAL ADVICE is important. All statements concerning arrests, charges and rulings that raise questions of libel or invasion of privacy should be examined by legal experts on our own staff, and in cases of heavy legal content the management will arrange to send copy to a consultant. See epithets, gender bias, physical appearance.

fall or *autumn*

faraway, but *You are far away.*

Farm Belt

far-off, but *The date is far off.*

farther refers to physical distances: *She threw the ball farther.* Further refers to abstract relationships of degree or quantity; it also means more or additional: *He had further reasons.*

Far West. See political regions.

faze/phase. Faze is to disturb or disconcert. As a noun, phase is a stage; as a verb, it means to introduce in stages.

FBI is acceptable on first reference if the meaning is clear.

Feb. See dates, months.

federal. Capitalize in a name; lowercase otherwise: *Federal Communications Commission, federal Department of Labor, federal employees, federal budget*.

Federal Register. Italicize. See titles of works.

F

fellow. Lowercase: *Nieman fellow,* but *Nieman Fellowship*.

fellow man. See gender bias.

fellowship. Capitalize in the name of an award; lowercase alone: *a Nieman Fellowship, the fellowship, a Nieman fellow*.

fewer measures numbers, not volume: *fewer birds, less corn*. When writing about ratios and percentages, use *fewer* when dealing with things that can be counted, less when dealing with quantity: *fewer than 1 in 10 editors, fewer than 50 percent of the company's employees, less than 50 percent of the company's work force*.

figure. Capitalize with a number or a letter: *Figure IV, Figure B, the figure*.

figures. See numbers.

fire-hardened

fire resistance

fire-resistant

first class (noun and adverb), *first-class* (adjective)

first come, first served; *first-come–first-served* policy

first family. *first lady, first cat*, etc.

firsthand. *firsthand information; They got the information firsthand,* but *at first hand*.

first in, first out; *first-in–first-out* system

first person. See we.

flair/flare. Flair is an ability or an artistic style; flare is to flame or to curve outward.

flaunt/flout. Flaunt is to show off; flout is to show contempt for.

fleet. Capitalize in a name; lowercase alone: *6th Fleet, Atlantic Fleet, the U.S. fleet (the fleet)*.

flextime

flier for pamphlets and pilots

flight. Capitalize with a number; lowercase alone: *Pan Am Flight 171, Flight 171 (the flight)*.

Florida (Fla., FL in addresses)

Floridian

flout. See flaunt/flout.

fly swatter

f.o.b. Abbreviation for free on board.

( )fold. *twofold, threefold, 12-fold, 50-fold*. When 10 grows twofold, it becomes 20; when 10 grows fourfold, it becomes 40.

following. Correct as an adjective: *The talk following the luncheon was mesmerizing.* Incorrect as an adverb: *He talked following the meeting.* Make it *He talked after the meeting.*

foot, feet. Abbreviate, *ft.,* only in charts, tables and maps.

foot dragging

footnotes. Use footnote symbols in this sequence:
*
†
**
‡
Notes and footnotes end with periods, even when no sentence is formed. Source lines do not. See charts and tables.

forbear/forebear. Forbear is to refrain; forebear is an ancestor.

fore( ). Write solid except before capitalization or an *e*.

forego/forgo. Forego is to precede; forgo is to relinquish.

foreign. When referring to the world at large, be sensitive to the fact that *international* may be preferable to *foreign,* which often implies antipathy or antagonism.

foreign currencies. See currencies.

foreign names. See Arabic names, Brazilian names, Chinese names, French names, German names, particles, Portuguese names, Russian names, Spanish-language names and the electronic NAMES and PLACES lists.

foreign officials, titles of. See titles of persons.

Foreign Service

foreign words. Italicize them when they are designated as such in the dictionary. If you use a word not in the dictionary but known to you as foreign, italicize it, too, unless it is a proper noun. See German common nouns, italics.

foreword/forward. Foreword is a preface; forward means toward the front or an offensive player in various sports.

forgo. See forego/forgo.

form. Capitalize with a number or a letter: *Form 1040, Form B (the form)*.

Fort. Do not abbreviate except in maps, charts and tables.

Fortune 500. Italicize ***Fortune*** but not *500:* ***Fortune*** *500.*

forward. See foreword/forward.

foundation. Capitalize in a name; lowercase alone: *the John D. and Catherine T. MacArthur Foundation (the MacArthur Foundation, the foundation)*.

Founding Fathers. Capitalize only when referring to Alexander Hamilton et al.

401(k), *401(k)'s*

fractions. Spell out and hyphenate when a fraction is used as an adjective and not part of a larger figure: *It was two-thirds gone*. Do not hyphenate when used as a noun: *He buried one third of the total*. When the denominator itself is hyphenated, drop the hyphen between the numerator and the denominator: *four twenty-fifths*. When a fraction is added to a number, use figures for the entire number: *2½ days*. If the fraction added to another number is other than one of those available on your keyboard (currently ⅛, ¼, ⅜, ½, ⅝, ¾, ⅞), write it with a space and a virgule, *6 13/16,* and flag it so the Composition Desk will close up the space and reduce the fraction to proper size.

(-)free. *duty-free goods; These goods moved duty free; tax-free bonds; These bonds are tax free.*

free world. Don't use except in quotes. Use a specific geographical term or "non-Communist world," if that is what is meant.

freight carloadings

french doors

french dressing

french-fried onion rings

french fries

french leave

French names. Follow the individual's preference on spelling and capitalization of personal names. *La, Le, Les* are usually capitalized: *Maurice de La Gorce (the La Gorce story, La Gorce). Des* and *Du* are usually capitalized if they occur at the start of a surname: *Pierre Du Pre (Du Pre), Armand Dupre (Dupre).* But watch out for double surnames. They raise questions not only of capitalization but of recognition; you have to be sure you do not mistake the first half of a double surname for a given name. An interior particle is likely to be lowercase: *Bernard Reynold du Chaffaut (Reynold du Chaffaut).* The contraction *d'* and *de* are usually lowercase. See particles.

Friends, Religious Society of. Shorten to *the Society of Friends* on subsequent mention or to *Friends* in such subsequent references as *the Friends' attitude toward war.* The Friends also may be called Quakers. The Society of Friends operates through five main groups: Friends General Conference, Friends United Meeting, Evangelical Friends Alliance, Religious Society of Friends (Conservative) and Religious Society of Friends (Unaffiliated Meetings). There are also some smaller unaffiliated groups. A local congregation is a *monthly meeting,* capitalized when part of a name. Some monthly meetings have no clergymen; others have leaders called pastors or executive secretaries: *John P. Piluk, pastor of Oak Grove Friends Meeting.* Monthly meetings are organized into quarterly or half-yearly meetings, and these are grouped into yearly meetings, which correspond to dioceses in some other denominations. These terms are capitalized when used in names. Quarterly or half-yearly meetings and yearly meetings are run by officials with the title of clerk: *Frank Konkus, clerk of the Center City Yearly Meeting.* The Society of Friends maintains contacts with the meetings (congregations) of the major organizations through the Friends World Committee for Consultation, to which they send delegates or observers.

front line (noun), *front-line* (adjective)

full-time. *They have full-time jobs. They are working full time.*

further is concerned with abstract relationships of degree or quantity. It also means more or additional *(further considerations); farther* is concerned with physical distances *(running farther)*.

fuse/fuze. Fuse is a general term for circuit breakers and devices to set off explosives; fuze is a device used to detonate ordnance.

'I weave my aesthetic instincts with the principles and purposes of communication on the loom of journalism, hoping each will serve the other as they pass imperceptibly into one another.'

RICHARD GAGE
GRAPHIC ARTIST

gallon(s). Abbreviate, *gal.,* only in charts, maps and tables.

gantlet/gauntlet. A gantlet is a section of overlapping railroad track or a punishment involving running between rows of hitters; a gauntlet is a glove. *To throw down the gauntlet* is to issue a challenge.

GAO. Acceptable on second reference to General Accounting Office.

GATT. Acceptable on second reference to General Agreement on Tariffs and Trade.

gay (noun and adjective). Acceptable for references to male and female homosexuals when the meaning is clear. **See homosexual, lesbian.**

GDP. Acceptable on second reference to gross domestic product.

Gen. *Gen. Mason Cunnion (General Cunnion, the general).* **See military titles.**

gender bias. Consider alternatives to language that emphasizes a person's sex or that implies certain occupations are in the exclusive domain of men or of women, that betrays surprise at finding, for example, a woman in a professional or executive position or a man in the nursing or nurturing field. Avoid feminine agent nouns, such as poetess, whose very existence often implies that the masculine form is the standard and the feminine form is exceptional.

Limiting Terms That May Be Offensive	Possible Alternatives
anchorman, anchorwoman	anchor
businessman, businesswoman	businessperson, business executive
businessmen	businesspersons, business people
career woman	(name the job or profession)
chairman	chair, chairperson, presiding officer
coed (noun)	student
comedienne	comedian
councilman	council member
craftsman	craftsperson, artisan
eight-man board	eight-member board, eight-person board
fireman	firefighter
fisherman	fisher, angler
foreman	supervisor
garbage man	garbage collector
housewife	homemaker
layman	layperson
mailman	letter carrier, postal worker
male nurse, model	nurse, model
man and wife	husband and wife
patrolman, policeman	police officer
poetess	poet
salesman	salesperson
sculptress	sculptor
stewardess	flight attendant, steward
woman lawyer	lawyer

Such dictionary-sanctioned words as *chairperson* and *spokesperson* are acceptable, but do not coin *-person* words. Consider alternatives to language that identifies the male as the archetype of the human race. Substitutions need not always be made when the cure would be worse than the disease.

Words Objected To	Possible Substitutes
fellow man	fellow human, fellow citizen
man, mankind	humankind, humanity, the human race, people
man's accomplishments	human accomplishments
man's spirit	the human spirit
workingman	worker, wage earner
the man for the job	the person for the job
man-made	artificial, synthetic, machine-made, handmade
the common man	ordinary people
one man, one vote	one person, one vote

Avoid language that stereotypes women as sex objects, cute, scatterbrained, timorous, shrewish, etc., and men as chauvinistic, loutish, insensitive, rude, etc. For additional help, consult *The Handbook of Nonsexist Writing* by Casey Miller and Kate Swift (Harper & Row, 1988). **See epithets, fairness, he/she, man.**

general. Capitalize before a name; lowercase otherwise. Abbreviate before full name; spell out otherwise: *Gen. Les Hall (General Hall, the general)*. **See military titles.**

General Assembly. Capitalize when referring to the name of a state or national governing body and to the United Nations body; lowercase general references: *the U.N. General Assembly (the General Assembly, the Assembly), the Arkansas General Assembly (the General Assembly, the Assembly). Usually, general assemblies are bicameral.*

G

geographic names. For spelling and capitalization, use the following references, in this order:

1. This stylebook, including the electronic PLACES list.
2. National Five-digit ZIP Code & Post Office Directory (National Information Data Center).
3. Webster's New World Dictionary, Third College Edition (Simon & Schuster, 1988).
4. Webster's New Geographical Dictionary (Merriam-Webster, 1988).
5. National Geographic Atlas of the World. (When a name in this atlas is followed by one with a different spelling in parentheses, *U.S. News* generally uses the one in parentheses; for example, *Lisbon* instead of *Lisboa*).
6. Columbia Lippincott Gazetteer of the World.

See nations and regions and the electronic PLACES list.

geographic terms. Capitalize places, real or imaginary, with special names: *the Delta, Badlands, Southern Highlands, Death Valley, Big Bend, Everglades, Panhandle, Black Hills, Rockies, Smokies, Black Forest, Upstate New York, Twin Cities, Border States, the Downs, the Promised Land, Lake District* (England). **See central, compass directions and individual entries, such as island, river, etc., and the electronic PLACES list.**

Georgia (Ga., GA in addresses)

Georgian

German common nouns. If they are used as foreign words, italicize them, lowercase. If the dictionary indicates they are anglicized, set them roman, lowercase.

German names. Use the diphthongs *ae, ie, oe* or *ue* only if you know that to be the way the individual's name is spelled; if the name uses an umlaut, use the umlaut; don't substitute the extra *e: Wolfgang von Goethe* (that's the way it's spelled), *Erich Spätmann* (if he spells it that way; not *Spaetmann*).

Germany. When referring to the formerly separate nations and cities, use *East Germany, West Germany, East Berlin* and *West Berlin*. When referring to sections of the unified nation, use *eastern Germany, western Germany, east Berlin* and *west Berlin*. Capitalize *East* and *West* when standing alone and referring to the former nations as well as to the post-unification sections: *Development in the East has not reached projections made in 1990.*

gerunds. See apostrophe.

ghetto(s). Avoid overuse when referring to an area where poor people or minorities live. *Section, area, district* and *slum* (if that is what is meant) often are better alternatives.

GI (GIs). Lowercase s even in all-caps headlines.

gibe/jibe. Gibe is to sneer; jibe is to be in agreement.

GI Bill. (An exception to the general rule on *bill*.) See bill.

girl. Do not use for females 18 and older.

GM. Acceptable for General Motors after spelling it out once. It may be used on first reference when the context makes its meaning clear.

GNP. Acceptable on second reference to gross national product.

God. See deity.

( )goer. Combines solid except when an awkward combination would result: *operagoer, theatergoer, Mardi Gras goer, strawberry-festival-goer*.

goodbye

Good Friday

goodwill

GOP. Acceptable as a synonym for Republican Party after first reference.

gorillas/guerrillas. Gorillas are animals; guerrillas are fighters.

got/gotten. The British never use *gotten*. Americans use both *got* and *gotten*, generally preferring *gotten* but often using *got* when used to mean "being in possession of" (*I have got the money*) and *gotten* when used to mean "have obtained" (*I have gotten plenty of money*). Using more-precise verbs (or just dropping *got*) can often do a better job: *I have the money. I received the money.*

government. Lowercase except in a name: *the U.S. government, the federal government, the Italian government, Government Employees Insurance Co., Government Printing Office.*

governor. Capitalize and abbreviate before a full name. Spell out with last name only. Lowercase alone: *Gov. Teresa Lauch (Governor Lauch, the governor)*. But spell out and lowercase when used with persons other than governmental chief executives: *Federal Reserve governor Calvin Hill.*

(-)grade. *first-grade pupil, 10th-grade student, low-grade uranium.*

grader. *first grader, 10th grader.*

G

grades. Capitalize, no quotes: *She got an A minus. Two B's were enough.* Plus and minus signs are acceptable when the meaning is clear: *Ashley received an A+ on her term paper.*

graduate. *She graduated from Trinity* is preferred. *She was graduated from Trinity* is acceptable. Do not write *She graduated Trinity* or *She graduated college.*

gram(s). Spell out on first reference. Abbreviation, *g,* is acceptable on second reference and in charts and tables.

gray

Great Britain, or Britain, is composed of England, Scotland and Wales. The United Kingdom is Britain and Northern Ireland. The British Isles consist of Britain, Ireland and adjacent islands, including the Isle of Man and the Channel Islands.

greater than, as great as. They don't mean the same thing. If Andy makes $50,000 a year and Amy makes $200,000, Amy's salary is four times as great as Andy's and three times greater than Andy's. The same kind of problem exists with "times more," "times higher" and "times larger." *Times smaller* is mathematically impossible; use a percentage or fraction instead.

great-grandfather, *great-great-grandfather, great-great-great-grandmother, six greats-grandmother* (the mother of a person's great-great-great-great-great-grandmother)

grounds. Use the plural when it means basis or foundation.

groundswell

group. Capitalize in a name or with a letter or a number: *the Cotter Advertising Group, Group W, Group A2, the Group of Seven industrialized nations (G-7).*

groups, names of.

actors	troupe
ants	colony
bees	swarm
birds	flight
chickens	flock
fish	school
geese	flock, gaggle
goats	flock, herd
hens	flock
horses	team
hounds	pack
insects	swarm
lions	pride
monkeys (large group)	troop
monkeys (small group)	gang
pigs	drove
porpoises	school
quail	bevy, covey
rabbits	warren
sheep	flock, herd
whales	pod
witches	coven
wolves	pack

guarantee. Use *guaranty* only in names that spell it that way.

Guard. See National Guard.

guerrillas. See gorillas/guerrillas.

gulf. Capitalize when part of a name; lowercase otherwise: *Gulf of Suez (the gulf), Persian Gulf (gulf states), Gulf of Mexico (the gulf,* but *Gulf States,* meaning Alabama, Florida, Louisiana, Mississippi and Texas).

guns. See weapons.

H

'Destiny is made, not found.'

JENNIFER HOWARD
NEWS BUREAU COORDINATOR

Hades, but lowercase *hell.*

hail/hail from/hale. hail (an ice pellet; to greet, call out, name by way of tribute); hail from (to come from); hale (to pull forcibly). *Hail fell while they hailed her as victor; she hailed a taxi; he hailed from Cedar City; she was haled into court.*

half(-). Follow the dictionary on whether to make combinations two words, solid or hyphenated (*half dollar, halfback, half-hour*). Combinations not in the dictionary are generally two words when used as a noun (*half century, half dozen, half mile*), hyphenated when used as an adjective (*half-century, half-dozen, half-mile*).

hand drill (noun), *hand-drill* (adjective and verb)

(-)handed. Hyphenate made-up combinations: *awkward-handed.*

handicap. Don't use to mean disability. A person with a disability who uses a wheelchair, for instance, is handicapped by a stairway. The person is disabled; the stairway is the handicap. **See disabled, victim.**

handyman, but *He is a handy man in a fight.*

Hanuka

hard-pressed. *It is a hard-pressed species,* but *the species is hard pressed.*

Hawaii (HI in addresses; otherwise do not abbreviate)

Hawaiian

HDR (HDRs). Acceptable on second reference to *humanitarian daily ration(s).*

headlines. Figures may be used in headlines for numbers of any size, but be consistent within a headline: *3 VISITS YIELD 13 SALES.* Use single quotes in headlines and decks, double quotes in precedes and subheads. Use en dashes (–) in headlines and decks, em dashes (—) in precedes. Don't use nicknames or first names of persons just to save space in a headline. When headlines are reprinted in an article, small caps, without quotation marks, may be used for effect, but in letters to the editor, write story titles in caps and lowercase, with quotation marks. UP-STYLE HEADLINES. In headlines and subheads that use "up" style, capitalize all words except the articles *a, an,* and *the;* the conjunctions *and, but, or, as* and *if,* and prepositions of three letters or fewer. Capitalize adverbs that form an integral part of a verb: *Japan Holds On to Islands, Taking Off for Australia, Jumping Up and Down, Potter Ran Up a Tab,* but *Duschene Ran up the Road* (*up* is a preposition). Capitalize the first and last words of such headlines, including articles, conjunctions and prepositions, no matter how short they are.

head-on (adjective and adverb). *a head-on crash; the candidates met head-on.*

headquarters is plural, but it often takes a singular verb: *The headquarters is in St. Louis.*

head to head. *They stood head to head,* but *a head-to-head confrontation.*

heaven

heavenly bodies. Planets, stars, constellations, etc., are capitalized; the generic portions of the names are generally lowercase: *the constellation Cassiopeia, Arcturus, Satellite VII of Jupiter, Mars's moon Phobos (Phobos, one of Mars's moons), Halley's comet, the Crab nebula, the Magellanic clouds.*

hectare. Abbreviation, *ha,* acceptable after first reference and in charts and tables.

hedging. When dealing with breaking news, pay particular attention to tenses and qualifying phrases so that the article will not sound silly because of something that happens over the weekend. See this week.

height. Use figures. *She was 5 feet, 2 inches tall; a 5-foot, 2-inch woman; she is 5 foot 2; a 5-foot-2 guard.* Acceptable when the meaning is clear: *Las Vegas's point guard stood 5-2.*

hell, but *Hades*

hemisphere. *the Western Hemisphere (the hemisphere).*

her, hers, she. Do not use for countries, ships or hurricanes. Use *it, its*.

herculean. Lowercase except when referring to Hercules.

hertz (Hz). See metric system.

he/she. With ingenuity, most sentences can be gracefully reworded to avoid such constructions as *he or she, him or her* and *his or hers.* When they cannot, use the masculine pronoun when an indefinite antecedent could be male or female. Helpful suggestions for avoiding he/she constructions can be found in *The Handbook of Nonsexist Writing* by Casey Miller and Kate Swift (Harper & Row, 1988). See fairness, gender bias.

hideout (noun)

high court. Acceptable on second reference to Supreme Court. See Supreme Court.

highflier, highflying

high mass is sung, not held. See mass.

high rate of speed is redundant. Write *high speed* unless you mean acceleration, which is the rate of increase in speed.

high school (noun and adjective)

high tech (noun), *high-tech* (adjective)

highway names. For interstate highways: *Interstate 15, the interstate*. On second reference, *I-15* is acceptable. For other federal highways: *U.S. 87*. For state and local highways: *Route 611, the route*. For roads that use the designation "Highway": *Highway 1A, the highway.*

Hill. Capitalize when it refers to Capitol Hill, but avoid overuse, which sounds jargonistic.

Hispanic is acceptable as a noun and as an adjective referring to persons tracing their descent to Latin America, Spain or Portugal: *a Hispanic*. Caution: Some Hispanics are black and some are white, so don't write, for example, *Hispanics and whites*. Use instead *Hispanics and non-Hispanics* or, if further distinction is needed, for example, *Hispanics and non-Hispanic whites*. See Chicano, ethnic identification, Latino.

historic. Use *a historic*.

historic events. Many easily recognized events are capitalized: *Boston Tea Party, Battle of Bull Run, the Long March*. Follow the dictionary and individual entries in this book and in the electronic NAMES file. If there is a possibility the term will not be understood, it probably should be lowercased and explained.

historic periods. Capitalize recognized terms: *Elizabethan Age, Jazz Era, Mauve Decade, Renaissance, Age of Reason, Roaring Twenties, Restoration, Christian Era,* but lowercase century: *20th century*. See ages and eras.

HIV (human immunodeficiency virus). Don't use the redundant *HIV virus*.

HMO(s). Acceptable on second reference to health maintenance organization(s).

hoard/horde. As a noun, a hoard is a stash; as a verb, it means to store away. A horde is a wandering group or a swarm.

hold down (verb), *hold-down* (noun and adjective)

holidays. Capitalize holidays, special days, special weeks, etc.: *Christmas, Easter Sunday, New Year's Eve, Christmas Eve, Hanuka, Good Friday, Holy Week, Passover, Ramadan, Lent, Independence Day, Fourth of July, Yom Kippur, Armistice Day, Mother's Day, Bastille Day, Veterans Day, Election Day, Inauguration Day, National Safety Week, Earth Week.*

Holy Communion. See sacraments.

holy orders

Holy Week

homeboy (noun, slang). Originally, someone from the same town, usually in the South. Now it also means a good buddy, friend or colleague. Use only when quoting someone.

home builder

home building (noun), *home-building* (adjective)

homesite

homosexual (noun and adjective). The term may be applied to both men and women. See gay, lesbian.

honorable, the. Abbreviate, *the Hon.*, before a full name. Use only in quoted matter.

honorific titles. Use the honorifics *Miss, Mr., Mrs.* and *Ms.* only in quoted matter or when needed for clarity, as when husbands and wives need to be distinguished from each other: *The Chubbs disagreed about little, although Mrs. Chubb favored decriminalization while Mr. Chubb supported prohibition*. (Alternatively, the tone of a story may allow you to make such a distinction using the couple's first names.)

hopefully means "in a hopeful mood": *He hopefully described the team's prospects.* Do not use it to mean "It is to be hoped." Incorrect: *She said that, hopefully, the team would win.*

horsepower. Abbreviation, *hp,* acceptable after first reference.

horse racing

hour(s). Abbreviate, *hr.,* only in charts, maps and tables. See time.

H

hourly-wage increase

House. Capitalize in reference to the U.S. House of Representatives and to a specific state's House of Delegates; lowercase as in *houses of Congress, either house of Congress*.

House of Commons *(the Commons, the House)*

hurricanes. Capitalize when personified: *Hurricane Hugo (the hurricane)*. Use *it,* not *he* or *she*.

husband. See wife, husband.

hyphen. There is wide disagreement over the many rules for hyphenation, and the exceptions often outnumber the rules. The guidelines below and those in the entry on compound words are aimed at promoting clarity without filling copy with unnecessary punctuation.
NATIONALITY COMBINATIONS: *Italian-American, Italian-Americans, Japanese-American, African-American, Afro-American,* but *Latin American, French Canadian*.
NUMBERS from twenty-one to ninety-nine, when spelled out (as at the beginning of a sentence), are hyphenated.
FRACTIONS. Hyphenate a fraction when it is used as an adjective: *two-thirds majority*. Write as two words when it is used as a noun: *two thirds of his fortune*.
X-TO-Y COMBINATIONS: *15-to-20-year-olds*. If these become too complicated, express them some other way: *persons 15 to 20 years old*.
COMPLEX VERBS. Follow the dictionaries on noun combinations used as verbs. Hyphenate made-up combinations:
You should horsewhip that fellow. (dictionary)
He blue-penciled my story mercilessly. (dictionary)
Jones three-putted the 19th hole. (made-up)

SUSPENDED HYPHENS. Put a space after the hyphen in such constructions as *they climbed the third- and fourth-highest peaks* and *she produced the video- and audiotapes*.
HOMOGRAPHS. Be alert to line breaks of words that have different pronunciations and meanings depending on how they are hyphenated: *re-cord* (verb), *rec-ord* (noun); *pro-ject* (verb), *proj-ect* (noun); *pro-gress* (verb), *prog-ress* (noun). Incorrect hyphenation can be fixed with the discretionary-hyphen key.
PREFIXES AND SUFFIXES are generally solid. Follow the dictionaries for words not in this book. For made-up words, hyphenate when a vowel would otherwise be doubled or a consonant tripled (*pre-empire, anti-inflation, bell-like,* but *cooperate and coordinate*); when sound or sense might be confused (*pro-union*); when a prefix is attached to a capitalized word (*pre-Columbian, trans-Atlantic*), and when a newly formed word resembles one with an established but different meaning (*work included re-creation of the old tavern; she re-covered the chair with burlap*). **See compound words, dash, fractions and entries for particular words, prefixes and suffixes.**

I

'The hours may be a little strange, but the people are great, and that's the best part of any job.'

TIM ITO
FACT CHECKER

I. See we.

ID. Acceptable for *identification* when the meaning is clear.

Idaho (ID in addresses. Otherwise abbreviate, *Ida.,* only in a tight spot on a map, chart or table.)

Idahoan

identification. Do not identify people by race, religion, national origin, ethnicity, etc., unless such identification is clearly pertinent to the story.

Il-76. Russian plane. See aircraft.

ill(-). As an adjective, it is usually hyphenated, even in the predicate: *Kristen made an ill-advised move. It was ill-advised.*

Illinois (Ill., IL in addresses)

Illinoisan

immigrate. *Troia immigrated to the United States; Arabet emigrated from Turkey.*

impact. Don't use as a verb except in quotes.

imply/infer. Imply is to indicate; infer is to draw a conclusion.

Impressionism. Capitalize references to the styles of art and music exemplified by, for example, Monet and Debussy; lowercase general references. See cultural designations.

Inauguration Day, but *inaugural address*

Inc. Do not set off by commas. It is not always needed. See company names.

inch(es). Abbreviate, *in.,* only in charts, maps and tables.

income-tax payer, but *taxpayer*

income tax return

independent counsel. This federal official was formerly called (and is still unofficially known as) a special prosecutor. Capitalize when used as a title before a name: *Independent Counsel Lawrence Walsh*. Titles of comparable state officials vary.

india ink

Indiana (Ind., IN in addresses)

Indianan

individual retirement account (IRA, IRAs). Abbreviation is acceptable on second reference.

Indochina, Indochinese

infantry. Capitalize in a name; lowercase otherwise: *1st Infantry Division (1st Infantry), the infantry, an infantry officer.*

infectious organisms. They are most often referred to by genus (capitalized) and species (lowercase): ***Staphylococcus aureus,*** both italicized. On second reference, the genus may be abbreviated: ***S. aureus***. Each such organism comes at the end of a long chain of classification, starting with phyla, which are divided into classes, then orders, families, genera and species. Classifications wider than genus will occur infrequently in news copy. When they do, they are capitalized but not italicized. The phylum Nematoda, for instance, is the overall group that includes in its chain the species ***Trichinella spiralis,*** cause of trichinosis.
Common names exist for some of these organisms, but not for others. The organ-

isms of ***T. spiralis,*** for example, may be referred to as trichinae, and Nematoda are nematodes. A strain is a variant that may be observed when the same species is isolated from different sources. If specimens of ***Streptococcus pyogenes*** taken from Doe and Roe show characteristics that are not the same, one may be called the Doe strain and the other the Roe strain. It takes a comprehensive medical dictionary to verify all the microorganisms that might appear in copy, but here are a few types to illustrate the forms. One reason for spelling out the genus on first appearance is the frequency with which the same initial stands for different genera:

Organism	Abbreviation
Bacillus anthracis (causes anthrax)	*B. anthracis*
Babesia bovis (infects cattle)	*B. bovis*
Escherichia coli (intestinal bacterium)	*E. coli*
Salmonella typhi (causes typhoid fever)	*S. typhi*
Salmonella choleraesuis (one of group causing food poisoning)	*S. choleraesuis*
Streptococcus pyogenes (causes strep throat)	*S. pyogenes*

To complicate matters, some bacteriologists use descriptive terms such as meningococcus, pneumococcus and typhoid bacillus, which are not part of the classification system. These are not ordinarily capitalized or italicized. They are usable words, and they can be checked in a medical dictionary or in the general dictionaries. Recommended: Stedman's Medical Dictionary, which is kept on the Fact Checkers' Desk, and Dorland's Illustrated Medical Dictionary.

infinitives. Don't hesitate to split one when doing so makes for easier reading or better understanding.

inflammable means the same as *flammable,* so use the shorter word.

infotainment

infra( ). Combines solid except before a capitalization or an *a*.

INF Treaty. Acceptable on second reference to Intermediate-range Nuclear Forces Treaty.

initials. When abbreviating parts of a name with letters, use a period: *T. Paul Urbach, J. R. Ewing, F. A. O. Schwarz,* putting a thin space between letters. But do not use periods after letters that are mere designations not standing for actual names: *A said to B; the X group accused the Y organization*. When using three initials in place of a name, make them solid: *FDR, JFK.* When using initials as a story credit, use a dash, periods and no spaces: *—R.J.N.*

institute. Capitalize in a name; lowercase alone. See colleges and universities.

insure. Use with regard to insurance. Use *ensure* when the meaning is "to make sure" or "make safe" and *assure* when the meaning is "to convince" or "to promise confidently."

inter( ). Combines solid except before a capitalization.

International Court of Justice. *World Court (the court)*.

Interstate. *Interstate 83, the interstate. I-83* is acceptable on second reference. See highway names.

intifada. Palestinian uprising in Gaza and the West Bank. Italicize.

intra( ). Combines solid except before a capitalization, before an *a* or in a confusing combination.

IOU (IOUs)

Iowa (IA in addresses. Otherwise abbreviate, *Ia.,* only in a tight spot on a map, chart or table.)

Iowan

IQ (IQs)

Iron Curtain

Islam. The Muslim religion. Members are Muslims, their deity is called Allah, Muhammad is the prophet and "messenger," the mosque is the house of worship and the holy day is Friday. Capitalize Prophet when it refers to Muhammad. Note: Although Arabic is the language of the Koran, the Islamic holy book, not all Arabs are Muslims and not all Muslims are Arabs. For instance, most Turks and Iranians are Muslims, but they are not Arabs. The two major groups in Islam are Sunni and Shiite. Leadership titles include imam, mullah, hojatoleslam, ayatollah, sheik and grand mufti. Organizations in the United States include the American Muslim Mission, which publishes the weekly *Muslim Journal* and whose leaders are addressed as *imam,* and the Nation of Islam, formerly the World Community of Islam in the West, which publishes the semiweekly *Final Call* and whose leaders are addressed as *minister*. See Muslim.

island. Capitalize when part of a name; lowercase otherwise: *Marianas Islands (the islands)*.

isotopes. Use a hyphen: *strontium-90, uranium-235*.

italics. TITLES. Italicize the names of books, newspapers, magazines, newsletters, plays, movies, operas, oratorios and other long musical compositions with distinctive names, ballets, paintings, sculpture, computer programs, collections of poetry and long poems published separately.

PERIODICALS. Italicize the names of newspapers, magazines and similar periodicals: ***Daily Citizen, U.S.News & World Report (U.S. News, USN&WR)***. Italicize and capitalize *the* only when the name is used formally or officially, as in photo credits and tables, and *the* is part of the periodical's name: ***The Capital Times*** (as a photo credit), *the* ***Capital Times*** or *the* ***Times*** (in body type). Italicize the name of the city only when the city is part of the official name: ***La Crosse Tribune,*** *the Baltimore* ***Sun***. Capitalize and italicize *magazine* only if the word is part of the title: ***New Orleans Magazine, Time*** *magazine*.

FOREIGN WORDS. Italicize those designated as such by Webster's New World Dictionary as well as common nouns not in the dictionary but known to you as foreign. Do not italicize foreign proper nouns.

FOR EMPHASIS. Using italics to stress a word is often a lazy way around good writing. Use the device sparingly.

A WORD REFERRED TO AS A WORD ONLY, not used for its meaning, is italicized: *He inserted an* ***and*** *into the record.*

LEGAL CITATIONS are italicized: ***Haley v. Oklahoma***.

PUNCTUATION marks generally take the font of the preceding word or character. Exceptions are parentheses and brackets.

POSSESSIVES. Set the apostrophe and the s roman: ***U.S. News***'s *ethical guidelines*. See book titles, computer programs, magazines, musical compositions, newspapers, titles of works.

its, it's. *Its* is the possessive of *it; it's* is the contraction for *it is: It's easy to find your car when you spot its antenna*. Do not use *it's* for *it has*.

J

'Style concerns what we omit and what we admit. Production aims to omit technical and logistical problems to admit into print the work of our literary and artistic colleagues.'

DIANE SNOW JAVAID
PRODUCTION MANAGER

jail. Do not use interchangeably with prison. In general, jails house persons who are awaiting trial or sentencing, who have been convicted of misdemeanors or who are confined for civil violations; prisons house convicted felons.

Jan. See dates, months.

jargon. See slang, dialect and jargon.

jeep. Lowercase generic descriptions of small military vehicles; capitalize when used as a trademark for Chrysler Corp. vehicles.

Jehovah. See deity.

Jewish congregations belong to one of three separate groups:
1. Union of American Hebrew Congregations (a Reform group)
2. United Synagogue of Conservative Judaism (a Conservative group)
3. Union of Orthodox Jewish Congregations of America (an Orthodox group)

Jewish houses of worship are called temples or synagogues. Reform congregations generally use temple: *Temple Beth El (the temple,* but check the individual name). Conservative congregations generally use synagogue: *Beth Israel Synagogue (the synagogue,* but check the individual name). Orthodox congregations always use synagogue: *Agudas Achim Synagogue (the synagogue).* Titles are rabbi and cantor: *Rabbi Samuel Silver (Rabbi Silver, Silver, the rabbi); Cantor Ralph Orloff (Cantor*

Orloff, Orloff, the cantor). Rabbinical groups: Central Conference of American Rabbis (Reform), Rabbinical Assembly (Conservative), Rabbinical Council of America (Orthodox) and Union of Orthodox Rabbis (Orthodox).

jibe. See gibe/jibe.

job-hopper

job-hopping

job preference

job seeker

Joint Chiefs of Staff, *Joint Chiefs, the chiefs of staff, the chiefs*

Jr. Do not set off with commas: *Robert Seeger Jr. went to the ocean.* Generally, it is not necessary to use *Jr.* unless there is the danger of confusion between a living father and son or when a person is well known by the *Jr.*

judge. Capitalize before a name; lowercase otherwise: *Appeals Court Judge Thomas Heep (appellate Judge Heep, federal Judge Heep, Judge Heep, the judge)*.

July. Do not abbreviate except in charts and tables. See dates, months.

June. Do not abbreviate except in charts and tables. See dates, months.

junk bonds

junk mail

juris doctor (J.D.) is the basic law school degree, which formerly was usually the bachelor of laws degree (LL.B.). Other law degrees include master of laws (LL.M.), master of comparative law (M.C.L.) and doctor of juridical science (S.J.D.). The doctor of laws degree (LL.D.) is often an honorary degree.

just( ). Do not hyphenate such constructions as *a just completed project, a just published study*.

justice. Capitalize before a name; lowercase otherwise: *Associate Justice Sandra Day O'Connor (Justice Sandra Day O'Connor, Justice O'Connor, the associate justice, the justice)*.

'Information is our game. Librarians know where it's at, what it's about, who it's for, when it's needed, how it's found and why it matters.'

JUDY KATZUNG
MANAGER, LIBRARY
NEWSPAPER SECTION

Kansan

Kansas (Kan., KS in addresses)

karaoke. Japanese for "empty orchestra," it is an electronic system that lets people sing along with popular musical selections. Set roman.

K.C. Its use as a nickname for Kansas City should generally be limited to quotes.

keep-away (noun)

( )keeper. Most combinations are solid, but some are two words. Follow the dictionaries: *bookkeeper, gatekeeper, hotelkeeper, housekeeper, peacekeeper, vigil keeper, record keeper, zookeeper.*

kente. Also *kente cloth*. A colorful fabric of Ghanaian origin, often worn as a symbol of African-American pride.

Kentuckian

Kentucky (Ky., KY in addresses)

Keogh plan(s)

kidnapping

kilobyte(s). Abbreviation, *K,* acceptable after first reference and in charts and tables: *260 kilobytes, 260K*.

kilogram(s). Abbreviation, *kg,* acceptable after first reference and in charts and tables.

kilometer(s). Abbreviation, *km,* acceptable after first reference and in charts and tables.

kilopascal(s). Abbreviation, *kPa,* acceptable after first reference and in charts and tables.

kilowatt(s). Abbreviation, *kW,* acceptable after first reference and in charts and tables.

kilowatt-hour(s). Abbreviation, *kWh,* acceptable after first reference and in charts and tables.

king. Capitalize before a name; lowercase alone. Use roman numerals: *King Bruno III (the king)*.

knock down (verb), *knockdown* (noun and adjective)

knot stands for nautical miles per hour, so don't write *knots per hour.*

Koran. See Islam.

kudos is singular.

'For me, a good artist is constantly curious and observant about everyday surroundings. I store these observations in my mind and use what I've learned to create art.'

ROD LITTLE
GRAPHIC ARTIST

L.A. is acceptable on second reference to Los Angeles when the meaning is clear.

La, Le, Les. See French names, particles.

Labrador. Abbreviate, *Lab.,* only in charts, maps and tables.

lady. Do not use as a synonym for *woman*.

lame duck (noun), *lame-duck* (adjective)

laptop computer

Latin American. Resident and adjective.

Latino is objectionable to some persons of Latin descent but is the term of choice for others; the generally preferred term is Hispanic. See Hispanic.

Latter-day Saints/Latter Day Saints. The original Mormon church uses a hyphen; the Reorganized Church of Jesus Christ of Latter Day Saints does not. See Mormons.

law. Lowercase, even in a name: *the immigration and nationality law,* but *Corn Laws* (because it's a historical term).

law degree. See juris doctor.

law school. See colleges and universities.

lectern/podium. A lectern is a stand that holds a speaker's notes; a podium is a platform that a speaker stands on.

left. Lowercase unless it is part of the official name of a political party: *the left wing of the party, a left-wing caucus.* Don't use *left-winger* except in quoted matter.

left-handed

legal advice. See fairness.

legal citations. Italicize: ***Brunowski v. Minnesota***.

legislature. Capitalize when it is the actual name of the body; lowercase otherwise: *Idaho Legislature (the Legislature), Massachusetts legislature* (the actual name is the General Court), *the Kansas and Florida legislatures*.

lesbian. Lowercase in references to homosexuals. See gay, homosexual.

less measures volume; *fewer* measures numbers: *less milk, fewer cows*. When writing about ratios and percentages, use less when dealing with quantity, fewer when dealing with things that can be counted: *less than 50 percent of the company's work force; fewer than 1 in 10 editors, fewer than 50 percent of the company's employees.*

liberal. Capitalize when referring to a political party; lowercase when designating a person's political position. Since the term often reflects the writer's individual judgment and may not correspond to another writer's interpretation or to a reader's, it is best to reserve it for cases in which there is widespread agreement. Where feasible, be more specific: *Senator Nickerson usually voted with the proponents of abortion funding*.

lieutenant governor. Capitalize and abbreviate before a full name; capitalize and spell out before a last name only; lowercase and spell out otherwise: *Lt. Gov. Lyle Betts (Lieutenant Governor Betts, the lieutenant governor)*.

life-size (adjective)

lift off (verb), *liftoff* (noun)

liftouts. See quotations.

like, as. Do not let the fact that *like* is often incorrectly substituted for *as* when introducing clauses keep you from using *like* as a perfectly good and often better substitute for *such as*. Correct: *Her voice sounds like a machine gun* (*like* is a preposition). *I feel well, as I knew I would* (*as* is a conjunction, introducing a clause. *Like* would be incorrect in place of *as*). *The table was full of goodies, like apples and candy* (*like* is as correct as *such as,* but it is more succinct).

( )like. As a suffix, write it solid except in cases of tripled *l (bell-like)* or after proper names *(Lincoln-like)*.

likely (adjective). *The Gophers are likely to win.* Do not use as an adverb unless it is preceded by *most, quite* or *very: He most likely will go*.

lists, enumerations. Treat alike all numbers of a group's elements:
First, the Celts. Second, the Saxons. Third, the Normans.
1. The United States did not sign the treaty.
2. Congress acted without responsibility.
These were the steps that led to peace: (1) establishment of the base at Subic Bay, (2) issuance of the U.S. ultimatum, (3) acceptance of the ultimatum.

liter(s). Abbreviation, *L,* acceptable after first reference and in charts and tables.

(-)lived. As a suffix, hyphenate: *long-lived*.

L

loath/loathe. Loath means reluctant; loathe means to detest.

locations. Capitalize special names of places, real and fanciful: *the Rockies, the Smokies, the Promised Land, Upstate New York, Twin Cities, the Panhandle, Camelot, Badlands*.

logon (noun); *log on* (verb)

( )long. *hourlong, daylong, nightlong, weeklong, monthlong, yearlong,* but *decade-long, century-long.*

long-term (adjective). *long-term advantage,* but *She did well in the long term.*

longtime (adjective). *longtime companions,* but *They lived together a long time.*

Louisiana (La., LA in addresses)

Louisianian

lower. See central.

lower 48. The contiguous states below the Canadian border.

low mass is recited, said or read, not sung or held. See mass.

LSD (the hallucinogen lysergic acid diethylamide). The abbreviation is acceptable on first reference if context makes the meaning clear.

Ltd. Do not set off with commas. It is not necessary to use *Ltd.* if Co., Corp., Railroad or other language clearly indicates a company name is used. See company names.

lunchtime

Lutherans in the United States are organized into two major groups: the Evangelical Lutheran Church in America and the Lutheran Church—Missouri Synod. They work together through the Committee on Lutheran Cooperation, but the committee has no governing power. The form for referring to Lutheran pastors of all groups: *the Rev. Henry Stromberg, pastor of First Lutheran Church (Pastor Stromberg, Stromberg)*. The Evangelical Lutheran Church in America is divided geographically into synods, headed by bishops. The Lutheran Church—Missouri Synod is divided into districts, headed by district presidents.

( )ly in multiple modifiers. When the first word is an adjective, use a hyphen; when it is an adverb, do not hyphenate: *settling the hourly-pay issue, reporting a stunningly decisive victory*.

M

'Journalism, at its best, is truth telling–or getting as close to that as humanly possible. That's what the care and precision of our guardians of style is all about.'

MERRILL MCLOUGHLIN
CO-EDITOR

( )made. Write solid if listed as such by the dictionary; hyphenate made-up combinations: *handmade, homemade, custom-made, factory-made, machine-made*.

magazines. Italicize the names of magazines. Capitalize and italicize *magazine* only when it is part of the official name of the publication: ***PC Magazine,*** but ***Time*** *magazine*. Capitalize and italicize *the* only when the name is used formally or officially, as in photo credits and tables, and it is part of the magazine's name: ***THE NEW REPUBLIC*** (as a photo credit), but *the* ***New Republic*** (in body type). See newspapers, titles of works.

Magna Carta

Maine (ME in addresses. Otherwise abbreviate, *Me.,* only in a tight spot on a map, chart or table.)

Mainer. A Maine resident or native.

majority. When it is used alone or with a prepositional phrase whose object is singular, it takes a singular verb: *The majority backs the president. A majority of the class goes on to college*. When the object of the prepositional phrase is plural, the verb may be singular or plural depending on the meaning: *A majority of the students go on to college,* but *A majority of two students sends the measure to defeat*.

majority leader. Capitalize as a title before a name; lowercase otherwise: *Senate Majority Leader Tom Gajewski (Majority Leader Gajewski; the Senate majority leader, Tom Gajewski)*.

major league (noun), *major-league* (adjective). Lowercase generic references to principal professional sports groups (*he was a major-league linebacker*), but capitalize trademarked references to baseball (*the Major Leagues, Major League Baseball*).

make over (verb), *make-over* (noun)

( )maker. Write dictionary-sanctioned words solid; make others two words: *speechmaker, bookmaker, diemaker, dressmaker, filmmaker, moviemaker, peacemaker, pacemaker, boilermaker, steelmaker, toolmaker, troublemaker, auto maker, carpet maker, decision maker, policy maker.*

make-work (noun and adjective)

Mall, the. Capitalize the one in Washington, D.C.; for all others, lowercase *mall* when standing alone.

man. Seek and use alternatives to *man* when the meaning includes women.

Traditional Expression	**Possible Alternative**
man the station	staff the station
man the barricades	mount the barricades
man should seek the truth	(people, we) should seek the truth
manpower	personnel, staff, work force, human resources
manpowered flight	human-powered flight, muscle-powered flight
workmanlike	skillful
man-day, man-hour	work-day, work-hour

See gender bias.

manila envelope, hemp, paper, rope, etc.

Manitoba. Abbreviate, *Man.,* only in charts, maps and tables.

Manitoban

mantel/mantle. A mantel is the facing around a fireplace, including a shelf above; a mantle is a cloak or cape.

maps. See captions; charts and tables.

March. See dates, months.

marine. If you could substitute the word *soldier, sailor* or *airman* for *marine,* make it lowercase: *15 marines began training*. Capitalize when referring to a particular country's organization: *the U.S. Marine Corps (the Marine Corps, the U.S. Marines, the corps, a Marine regiment, a Marine sergeant, 15 Marine recruits finished training), the French Marine Corps, the U.S. and French marine corps*. See military titles.

Maryland (Md., MD in addresses)

Marylander

Mason-Dixon Line

mass, high mass, low mass. Masses are not "held." Mass is celebrated, read or said. High mass is sung. Low mass is recited, said or read.

Massachusetts (Mass., MA in addresses)

Massachusetts resident, native, etc. Also acceptable are *Massachusettsan* and *Bay Stater.*

master of arts (M.A.), *a master of arts degree, a master's degree, a master's*

May. See dates, months.

M

mayor. Capitalize as a title before a name; lowercase otherwise: *Mayor Leonard Andrews (Mayor Andrews, the mayor), a mayor.*

mdse. Acceptable abbreviation for *merchandise* in maps, charts and tables.

MDT. See time zones.

meat-ax (noun and adjective)

meatcutter

meat grinder

meat wagon

medal. Capitalize with a specific name; lowercase for awards representing levels of victory in track meets, fairs, etc.: *the Medal of Honor, the Good Conduct Medal, silver medal in the pole vault.*

medevac helicopter

media. *Medium* is singular; *media* is plural: *The television medium is cool. The newspaper and magazine media are hot.*

Medicaid

medical terms. DISEASES, CONDITIONS AND SYMPTOMS are roman and lowercase except for proper names they may contain: *aneurysm, atherosclerosis, emphysema, Hodgkin's disease, hyperglycemia, infarction, measles, Ménière's syndrome, neuralgia, osteoarthritis, Parkinson's disease.*
TESTS AND TREATMENTS also are generally lowercase and roman except for words that would be capitalized when alone: *tuberculin test, barium X-ray, cobalt therapy, acupuncture, Heimlich maneuver, Pap smear, metabolism test.*
IN NONMEDICAL CONTEXTS, take care not to misuse terms (schizophrenia, for instance, is not the same as split personality), and be vigilant when using terms describing medical conditions in a nonmedical context—which can be unnecessarily painful to people with such conditions and to those close to them. See infectious organisms, handicap.

Medicare

medigap. Nickname for Medicare supplement insurance, which is designed to pay most medical expenses not covered by Medicare.

mega( ). Combines solid except before an *a: megabuck, megabyte, megadeath, megadose, mega-answer.*

megabyte (MB). *1 megabyte, 16 megabytes, 1MB, 16MB.*

member of Congress. See congressman.

member of Parliament (M.P.). Capitalize before a name; lowercase otherwise: *Member of Parliament Buddy Sanconis, the member of Parliament. M.P. Buddy Sanconis* is acceptable if the context makes the title clear.

merchant marine. *U.S. merchant marine, the merchant marine,* but *U.S. Merchant Marine Academy.*

meter(s). Abbreviation, *m,* is acceptable after first reference and in charts and tables.

Methodists. See United Methodist Church.

metric system. In general, use metric units when they are relevant in a story and would not confuse readers, as in technical references in articles about science and medicine. In nontechnical uses, however, readers are usually better served by traditional units, so when, for instance, a correspondent in Pretoria writes about hauling a 25-kilogram package along a 5-kilometer road, it is generally better to convert the weight to pounds and the distance to miles. In most cases, metric terms should be spelled out the first time they are used. Thereafter, abbreviation is acceptable if it suits the tone of the article. Metric abbreviations are not followed by a period. Some measures, such as those of guns, are abbreviated on first reference: *77-mm gun, 7.3-mm pistol.*

Name	Symbol	Approximate Size or Equivalent
Length		
meter	m	39½ inches
kilometer	km	.6 mile
centimeter	cm	width of a paper clip
millimeter	mm	thickness of a paper clip
Area		
hectare	ha	2½ acres
Weight		
gram	g	weight of a paper clip
kilogram	kg	2.2 pounds
metric ton	t	long ton (2,240 pounds)
Volume		
liter	L	one quart and 2 ounces
milliliter	mL	⅕ teaspoon
Pressure		
kilopascal	kPa	atmospheric pressure is about 100 kPa
Temperature		
Celsius	°C	5/9 °F after subtracting 32 from °F
freezing	0°C	32°F
boiling	100°C	212°F
body temp.	37°C	98.6°F
room temp.	20-25°C	68-77°F
Electricity		
kilowatt	kW	
kilowatt-hour	kWh	
megawatt	MW	
Miscellaneous		
hertz	Hz	one cycle per second
millisecond	ms	

CAPITALS. Names of all units start with a lowercase letter except at the beginning of a sentence. Exception: In *degrees Celsius, degrees* is lowercase but the modifier *Celsius* is capitalized. Symbols for units are lowercase except for liter and units derived from the name of a person (*m* for *meter* but *W* for *watt, Pa* for *pascal, Hz* for *hertz,* etc.). Symbols for prefixes that mean a million or more are capped and those for less than a million are lowercase (*M* for *mega, k* for *kilo*).

PLURALS. Names of units are made plural only when the numerical value that

precedes them is more than 1. For example, *0.25 liter* or *¼ liter,* but *250 milliliters*. Symbols for units are never pluralized (*250 mL*).
SPACING. Leave a space between the number and the symbol to which it refers *(7 m; 31.4 kg,* but *32°F, 260K* and *12MB)*.
PERIOD. Do not use a period with metric-unit names and symbols except at the end of a sentence.
CONVERSIONS. Follow reason: Don't include figures that imply more accuracy than justified by the original data. For example, 36 inches would be converted to 91 centimeters, and 40.1 inches would convert to 101.9 centimeters, not 101.854.
DETAILS. Further help is available in "NBS Guidelines for Use of the Metric System," a free booklet published by the National Institute of Standards and Technology.

Common Prefixes

Factor	**Prefix**	**Symbol**
1,000,000	mega	M
1,000	kilo	k (But cap *K* when it stands for kilobyte)
10	deka	da
1/10	deci	d
1/100	centi	c
1/1,000	milli	m
1/1,000,000	micro	(Use the Greek letter Mu, which is available in type but not on screen; alert the Composition Desk with a message and flag the top of the story. When the Greek Mu is not available, the letter *u* is an acceptable alternative.)

Metric Conversion Factors (approximate)

When you know length	**Multiply by**	**To find**	**Symbol**
inches	2.54	centimeters	cm
feet	30	centimeters	cm
yards	.9	meters	m
miles	1.6	kilometers	km
Area			
square inches	6.5	square centimeters	cm^2
square feet	.09	square meters	m^2
square yards	.8	square meters	m^2
square miles	2.6	square kilometers	km^2
acres	.4	hectares	ha
Weight			
ounces	28	grams	g
pounds	.45	kilograms	kg
short tons (2,000 pounds)	.9	metric tons	
teaspoons	5	milliliters	mL
tablespoons	15	milliliters	mL

When you know volume	Multiply by	To find	Symbol
cubic inches	16	milliliters	mL
fluid ounces	30	milliliters	mL
cups	.24	liters	L
pints	.47	liters	L
quarts	.95	liters	L
gallons	3.8	liters	L
cubic feet	.03	cubic meters	m^3
cubic yards	.76	cubic meters	m^3
Pressure			
inches of mercury	3.4	kilopascals	kPa
pounds/square inch	6.9	kilopascals	kPa
Temperature (exact)			
degrees Fahrenheit (after subtracting 32)	5/9	degrees Celsius	°C

(Explanations and tables in this section are taken from "Metric Style Guide for the News Media," published by the National Institute of Standards and Technology, with adjustments to accommodate *USN&WR* methods of writing and abbreviation.) See temperature, weights and measures.

metric ton. 1,000 kilograms (about 2,200 pounds). Abbreviation, *t,* acceptable after first reference and in charts, maps and tables.

Mexican-American. An American of Mexican origin.

Mexican names. See Spanish-language names.

mfg. Acceptable abbreviation for *manufacturing* in maps, charts and tables.

mfr., mfrs. Acceptable abbreviation for *manufacture* or *manufacturer(s)* in maps, charts and tables.

Michigan (Mich., MI in addresses)

Michigander, but *Michiganian traits* or *Michigan traits*

mid( ). Usually written solid unless followed by a capitalization or a figure: *midlife, midafternoon, midcentury, midocean, midrange, midseason, midsize, mid-Atlantic, mid-1980s, mid-'90s*.

middle. See central.

middle age (noun), *middle-aged* (adjective)

Middle Ages

middle America is an imprecise term at best. In general, limit its use to quotations. See exact words.

Middle East. Authorities differ on the boundaries. For general use, it comprises the countries from Iran to Asiatic Turkey, including Egypt, Cyprus and the Arabian Peninsula. Also sometimes included are Afghanistan, Sudan, Libya, Tunisia, Algeria and Morocco. See Near East.

Mideast. Acceptable for *Middle East*.

Midwest. See political regions.

MiG-25. See aircraft.

mil. Acceptable abbreviation for *million(s)* in charts, maps and tables.

mile. Do not abbreviate.

miles per gallon (mpg). Abbreviation is acceptable on all references.

miles per hour (mph). Abbreviation is acceptable on all references.

military police (MP, MPs)

military titles. Abbreviate before a full name and, if necessary, in charts; spell out otherwise. Capitalize before a name; lowercase otherwise. A military title may be dropped on subsequent reference, but it is frequently useful to keep it. Abbreviations for service designations, *USA (for U.S. Army), USNR (for U.S. Navy Reserve),* etc., are acceptable with full name and rank: *Lt. (j.g.) William Oliver, USNR*.

COMMISSIONED OFFICERS

Army, Marine Corps, Air Force

Name of rank	**Before full name**	**Before last name**	**In later mention**
General	Gen.	General	the general
Lieutenant General	Lt. Gen.	General	the general
Major General	Maj. Gen.	General	the general
Brigadier General	Brig. Gen.	General	the general
Colonel	Col.	Colonel	the colonel
Lieutenant Colonel	Lt. Col.	Colonel	the colonel
Major	Maj.	Major	the major
Captain	Capt.	Captain	the captain
First Lieutenant	1st Lt.	Lieutenant	the lieutenant
Second Lieutenant	2nd Lt.	Lieutenant	the lieutenant

Navy

Name of rank	Before full name	Before last name	In later mention
Admiral	Adm.	Admiral	the admiral
Vice Admiral	Vice Adm.	Admiral	the admiral
Rear Admiral	Rear Adm.	Admiral	the admiral
Rear Admiral (Lower)	Rear Adm.	Admiral	the admiral
Captain	Capt.	Captain	the captain
Commander	Cmdr.	Commander	the commander
Lieutenant Commander	Lt. Cmdr.	Commander	the commander
Lieutenant	Lt.	Lieutenant	the lieutenant
Lieutenant (junior grade)	Lt. (j.g.)	Lieutenant	the lieutenant
Ensign	Ens.	Ensign	the ensign

Maj. Gen. Jesse Aument (General Aument, Aument, the general)

Warrant Officers

Name of rank	Before full name	Before last name	In later mention
Chief Warrant Officer 2, 3 and 4	Chief Warrant Officer	Chief Warrant Officer	the warrant officer
Warrant Officer	Warrant Officer	Warrant Officer	the warrant officer

Chief Warrant Officer Kenneth Brown (Chief Warrant Officer Brown, Brown, the warrant officer)

ENLISTED RANKS

Army

Sergeant major of the Army follows the name: *Charles MacDowell, sergeant major of the Army (Sergeant MacDowell, MacDowell, the sergeant).*

Before full name	Before last name only
Command Sgt. Maj.	Sergeant
Staff Sgt. Maj.	Sergeant
1st Sgt.	Sergeant
Master Sgt.	Sergeant
Platoon Sgt.	Sergeant
Sgt. 1st Class	Sergeant
Staff Sgt.	Sergeant
Sgt.	Sergeant
Cpl.	Corporal
Spc.	Specialist
Pfc.	Private
Pvt.	Private

Command Sgt. Maj. Perry Sassoon (Sergeant Sassoon, Sassoon, the sergeant)

Marine Corps

Names of ranks in the Marine Corps follow the Army model and should be treated in the same way, although the named ranks do not always correspond.

Two exceptions:

Before full name	Before last name only
Master Gunnery Sgt.	Sergeant
Lance Cpl.	Corporal

Navy

Master chief petty officer of the Navy follows the full name: *John Paul Smith, master chief petty officer of the Navy (Chief Smith, Smith, the chief)*.

Before full name	Before last name only
Master Chief Petty Officer	Chief
Senior Chief Petty Officer	Chief
Chief Petty Officer	Chief
Petty Officer 1st Class	Petty Officer
Petty Officer 2nd Class	Petty Officer
Petty Officer 3rd Class	Petty Officer
Seaman	Seaman
Seaman Apprentice	Seaman
Seaman Recruit	Recruit

SPECIALTIES: The Navy and the Coast Guard have more than 75 types of specialists who are customarily referred to by their specialties. They range from boatswain's mate to electronics-warfare technician, and each specialty runs the scale of ranks from recruit to master chief. The hundreds of official abbreviations are meaningless to all but a few readers, so the only useful abbreviation is omission of a few words. Lowest rating of electronics-warfare technician, for instance, is *Electronics Warfare Technician Seaman Recruit Manny Langston,* but for our purposes he is *Seaman Recruit Manny Langston, an electronics-warfare technician (Seaman Recruit Langston, Langston, the seaman recruit)*. Taking radioman as an example, the ratings are:

Before full name	Before last name	In later mention
Master Chief Radioman	Chief	the chief
Senior Chief Radioman	Chief	the chief
Chief Radioman	Chief	the chief
Radioman 1st Class	Radioman	the radioman
Radioman 2nd Class	Radioman	the radioman
Radioman 3rd Class	Radioman	the radioman
Radioman Seaman	Seaman	the seaman
Radioman Apprentice	Apprentice	the apprentice
Radioman Recruit	Recruit	the recruit

Master Chief Radioman Bill Budd (Chief Budd, Budd, the chief)

Note: Specialists beginning with 3rd class hold the parallel ratings of petty officers, chief petty officers, etc.; nevertheless, they usually are styled by their specialties.

Air Force

Chief master sergeant of the Air Force follows the name: *Seth Wright, chief master sergeant of the Air Force (Chief Wright, Wright)*. Other ranks:

Before full name	**Before last name only**
Chief Master Sgt.	Chief
Senior Master Sgt.	Sergeant
Master Sgt.	Sergeant
Technical Sgt.	Sergeant
Staff Sgt.	Sergeant
Sgt.	Sergeant
Senior Airman	Airman
Airman 1st Class	Airman
Airman	Airman
Airman Basic	Airman

See retired.

military units. Use figures and capitalize long and short names: *101st Airborne Division (Air Assault), 101st Airborne Division, 101st Airborne, 6th Fleet,* but *the division, the airborne, the fleet*. Use roman numerals for Army corps: *V Corps, the corps*. Capitalize and put quotation marks around nicknames: *the "Screaming Eagles."*

millennium(s)

milliliter(s). Abbreviation, *mL,* acceptable after first reference and in charts and tables.

millimeter(s). Abbreviation, *mm,* acceptable after first reference and in charts and tables and in such familiar uses as *75-mm gun, 7.3-mm pistol*.

million. When using numbers in millions, billions or trillions, substitute the word for the zeros. Portions of a million, billion or trillion may be shown in decimals, but except where necessary to show fine distinctions, round to no more than one digit after the decimal point: *8 million, 18 million, 12.3 billion, 1.5 trillion*. If it is vital to go beyond one digit, up to three may be used. If exact numbers must be carried still further to show the desired information, use figures: *8,737,542; 7,346,507,000*. Do not hyphenate when amounts are used adjectivally: *a 15 million-gallon oil spill*.

millowner

(-)minded. *broad-minded, open-minded, narrow-minded,* etc.

mine owner, *minesweeper, mine worker*

mini( ). Write solid except before a capitalization, before an *i* or in a difficult-to-read combination: *minibus, minicar, miniskirt, ministate, mini-apology.*

minister. Capitalize as in *Finance Minister,* etc., before a name; lowercase otherwise: *Finance Minister Robert Feustal, the finance minister, finance ministers.*

Minnesota (Minn., MN in addresses)

Minnesotan

minority leader. Capitalize as a title before a name; lowercase otherwise.

minuscule

minute(s). Abbreviate, *min.,* only in charts, maps and tables. Spell out nine and below; use figures for 10 and above. See numbers.

MIRV (MIRVs). Abbreviation for multiple independently targeted (or targetable) reentry vehicle(s). Use only with an explanation.

Miss. See honorific titles.

missiles. See rockets.

Mississippi (Miss., MS in addresses)

Mississippian

Missouri (Mo., MO in addresses)

Missourian

MIT. Acceptable on second reference to Massachusetts Institute of Technology.

mixed metaphors. Avoid such combinations as: *They went where the hand of man has never set foot.*

model. Capitalize with number and/or letter: *Model 3C (the model).*

Mohammed. See Muhammadan.

M-1. A measure of the U.S. money supply. *M-1A, M-2,* etc.

money. Use figures for sums of money, except when they begin a sentence. They are usually treated as singular: *$4, $450, $4 million, 7 cents, a $4.3 million loan. Fifty thousand dollars was appropriated. About $50 million was stolen.* Change foreign currency to the equivalent in U.S. dollars where possible. See currencies.

( )monger. Combinations are one word: *warmonger, whoremonger, rumormonger.*

monsignor. *Msgr. Bruno Morawski (Monsignor Morawski, the monsignor).*

Montana (Mont., MT in addresses)

Montanan

month. Abbreviate, *mo.,* only in charts, maps and tables.

months. Use these abbreviations when they appear with a date and year: *Jan., Feb., Aug., Sept., Oct., Nov., Dec.* Do not abbreviate the month when standing alone or when used with the year only or the day only. In general, do not abbreviate months with five letters or fewer. But abbreviations or initial letters, where clear in meaning, may be used in charts, maps and tables. See dates.

monuments. Capitalize names: *Jefferson Memorial, Brandenburg Gate, the Statue of Liberty, Washington Monument (the monument).*

moon. See heavenly bodies.

more than. See over.

Mormons. The Church of Jesus Christ of Latter-day Saints may be referred to as the Mormon Church in first and subsequent mentions if the full name appears at least once in the article. Members may be referred to as Mormons or Latter-day Saints. A branch is a small congregation, a ward is a large congregation and a stake is a district made up of a number of congregations. There are two divisions of the priesthood: the Aaronic and the Melchizedek. The offices of the Aaronic priesthood, beginning with the lowest: deacon, teacher, priest and bishop. The offices in the Melchizedek priesthood are: elder, seventy, high priest, patriarch and apostle. A person of any ranking from elder up may be referred to as elder. *President Walter Beitz of the Riverdale Stake (Elder Beitz, Beitz). President John Smith of the Homeville Branch (President Smith, Elder Smith, Smith, the president* [equivalent to pastor]). *Bishop John Smith of the Centerton Ward (Bishop Smith, Elder Smith, Smith, the bishop* [equivalent to pastor]). At Mormon Church headquarters, the presiding officer is the first president. The first president and two counselors form the First Presidency; under the First Presidency is the Quorum of Twelve Apostles; under the Twelve is the First Quorum of Seventy. Any member of these groups may be referred to as elder: *Elder John Smith, an apostle and member of the Quorum of Twelve (Elder Smith, Smith).* An additional body is the Presiding Bishopric, composed of the presiding bishop and two counselors and reporting directly to the first president. The bishopric has responsibility for temporal affairs. Its members are addressed as Bishop: *Bishop Allison Young (Bishop Young, the bishop, Young).*
REORGANIZED CHURCH OF JESUS CHRIST OF LATTER DAY SAINTS (note *Latter*

Day has no hyphen) uses the same terminology for its officials but calls its divisions by slightly different names. Individual churches are missions, branches and congregations. Missions and branches are responsible to district presidents; district presidents report to regional presidents, and regional presidents to the Quorum of the Council of the Twelve Apostles. Congregations, which usually are larger groups and often urban, are organized into stakes, which are responsible to the Apostles.

Moslem. See Muslim.

most favored nation (noun), *most-favored-nation* (adjective)

Most Rev. *the Most Rev. Jimmy Jones (Archbishop Jones, the archbishop, Jones)*.

Mother's Day

Mount. Do not abbreviate except in maps, charts and tables.

mountain. Capitalize when part of a name; lowercase alone: *Rocky Mountains (the mountains), Sand Mountain (the mountain)*. Note: *sierra* means mountains, so don't write, for instance, *Sierra Nevada Mountains*. Write *Sierra Nevada, Sierra Nevada range, Sierras*.

Mountain states. See political regions.

movements. Lowercase except when they are derived from proper names: *democracy, communism, Marxism, Marxist, conservative thought, Conservative (Party) platform*.

moviemaking

movie ratings. *G, PG-13, PG, R, NC-17, movie rated R, an R-rated movie*.

movies, names of. Capitalize as the movie does and set in italics.

mox nix. Corruption of German es *macht nichts* (it doesn't matter). Don't use without an explanation.

MP(s). Acceptable on first reference to military police or military police officer(s) when the meaning is clear.

M.P. Member of Parliament. See member of Parliament.

mpg. Acceptable on all references to miles per gallon.

mph. Acceptable on all references to miles per hour.

Mr., Mrs., Ms., Miss. See honorific titles.

MREs. Acceptable on second reference to *meals ready to eat*.

MST. See time zones.

Muhammadan. Acceptable for references to the prophet Muhammad, but use *Muslim* or *Islam* in references to the religion.

mujeheddin. Islamic warriors.

multi( ). Write solid except before an *i* or a capitalization.

multimillion-dollar (adjective)

multiple modifiers. See hyphen, compound words.

musical compositions. Capitalize the main words. Use italics for the nontechnical parts of titles of long compositions: *Mozart's Symphony No. 41 in C Major, Mozart's* ***Jupiter*** *Symphony, Schubert's Eighth Symphony, Copland's* ***Appalachian Spring,*** *Bartok's Piano Concerto No. 3*. Use quotation marks for songs and names of albums: Harrison's *"Here Comes the Sun"; "Frankie Ford's Oldies but Goodies, Volume 3."* See titles of works.

Muslim. Use *Muslim* and *Islam,* not *Moslem* and *Muhammadan,* in references to the religion. Do not use the term *Black Muslim* except as a historical term or when quoting someone. See Islam.

mutual funds. The first source for a fund's name is the *Investor's Mutual Fund Guide,* from Investment Company Data. For a fund too new to be in the guide, which is updated monthly, use the particular fund's prospectus. The Investment Company Institute's annual *Guide to Mutual Funds* is a useful source for a fund's entire name.

FUND. Include *Fund* only when it helps identify a specific fund: *Janus Fund,* not *Janus,* but *Janus Twenty*. *Fidelity Fund,* but *Fidelity Magellan*.

FAMILY NAME. Include it in charts and tables and, unless it is otherwise clear from context, in running copy: *Fidelity Magellan,* not *Magellan*.

CATEGORIES. In describing a fund's type or its investment objective, use the categories in the *Investor's Mutual Fund Guide*. However, to save space, the *USN&WR* quarterly mutual fund chart uses slightly different categories.

ABBREVIATION. When fund names must be shortened, first drop nonessential words, then abbreviate, but never so much that identification of the fund becomes difficult: *Fidelity Select Portfolios Biotechnology Portfolio* could become *Fidelity Select Biotechnology* or, if space is especially tight, such as in charts or tables, *Fidelity Sel. Biotech.* (but not, for example, *Fid. Sl. Bio.*).

PUNCTUATION. Do not use colons, hyphens or dashes unless confusion could result otherwise: *Mutual Beacon,* not *Mutual: Beacon; Fidelity Select Health Care,* not *Fidelity Select-Health Care,* but *Oregon Tax-Exempt Series*. Use periods with abbreviations.

N

'I used to think you needed money to have style. Working here, I know otherwise.'

RICK NEWMAN
REPORTER

NAACP. Abbreviation for the National Association for the Advancement of Colored People may be used on first reference in a tight lead, but the name should be spelled out as soon as possible. See the electronic NAMES list.

names of persons. Use whatever name a person is known by, whether the name was received at birth, adopted legally or taken informally for professional purposes, such as a stage name, pen name or nom de guerre. When a newsworthy person changes names, use both names until readers become familiar with the new name. Use the spellings in this book and the electronic NAMES list, then consult the following:

1. Webster's New World Dictionary (Simon & Schuster).
2. Webster's New Biographical Dictionary (Merriam-Webster).
3. Who's Who in America and Who Was Who in America.
4. Current Biography, the Britannica and Americana encyclopedias and the Political Handbook of the World.

With foreign names, aid can be had from the country desks of the State Department, from the State Department's Diplomatic List and from the CIA's Chiefs of State and Cabinet Members of Foreign Countries. In using these sources, however, apply *U.S. News* rules for the country in question. Consult the electronic NAMES list for specific personal and company names. For the sake of clarity, capitalize initial letters even if the individual does not: *E. E. Cummings, K. D. Lang.* Do not use a person's given name alone in headlines or on second reference in a story unless there is a compelling reason to do so, such as if the person is very young or to distinguish brothers and sisters or spouses from one another. See Arabic names, Brazilian names, Chinese names, French names, German names, honorific titles, nicknames, particles, Portuguese names, Russian names, Spanish-language names and the electronic NAMES list.

NASA. Acceptable in a tight lead on first reference to the National Aeronautics and Space Administration, but spell it out at the earliest opportunity.

nation, national. Capitalize in a name; lowercase otherwise: *National Urban Coalition, the national government*.

National Assembly. Capitalize when it is the actual name of a body: *French National Assembly (the National Assembly, the Assembly)*. See assembly.

national chairman. Capitalize when used as a title before the name of a head of a political party; lowercase otherwise: *Democratic National Chairman Silas Evans, the Democratic national chairman*.

national committee. Capitalize in the full name of a political party's organization; lowercase otherwise: *the Republican National Committee (the GOP National Committee, the national committee, the committee)*.

national committeeman(woman). Capitalize as a title before a name; lowercase otherwise: *National Committeewoman Marianne Sunshine (the national committeewoman)*.

national convention of a political party. Capitalize in the full name; lowercase otherwise: *the Democratic National Convention (the Democratic convention, the national convention, the convention)*.

National Guard. Capitalize when referring to a particular state's or nation's organization: *the Utah National Guard (the National Guard, the Guard, a national guardsman, a guardsman)*.

nationality. See nations and regions.

National Safety Week

Nation of Islam. See Islam.

nations and regions. Spell out whenever possible. The following abbreviations may be used in tight situations, but only in maps, charts and tables.

Region	**Resident**	**Adjective**	**Abbreviation**
Afghanistan	Afghan(s)	Afghan	Afgh.
Albania	Albanian(s)	Albanian	Alb.
Algeria	Algerian(s)	Algerian	Alg.

Region	Resident	Adjective	Abbreviation
American Samoa	Samoan(s)	Samoan	Am. Sam.
Andorra	Andorran(s)	Andorran	And.
Angola	Angolan(s)	Angolan	Ang.
Anguilla (dependency of Britain)	Anguillan(s)	Anguillan	Angu.
Antigua & Barbuda	Antiguan(s) & Barbudan(s)	Antiguan & Barbudan	Ant., Barbu.
Argentina	Argentine(s)	Argentine	Arg.
Armenia	Armenian(s)	Armenian	Arm.
Aruba	Aruban(s)	Aruban	Aru.
Australia	Australian(s)	Australian	Austral.
Austria	Austrian(s)	Austrian	Aust.
Azerbaijan	Azerbaijani(s)	Azerbaijani	Azer.
Bahamas	Bahamian(s)	Bahamian	Bah.
Bahrain	Bahraini(s)	Bahraini	Bahr.
Bangladesh	Bangladeshi(s)	Bangladesh	Bngl.
Barbados	Barbadian(s)	Barbadian	Barb.
Belarus	Belarussian(s)	Belarussian	Bela.
Belgium	Belgian(s)	Belgian	Belg.
Belize	Belizean(s)	Belize	Belz.
Benin	Beninese	Beninese	Benin
Bermuda	Bermudan(s)	Bermudan	Berm.
Bhutan	Bhutanese	Bhutanese	Bhu.
Bolivia	Bolivian(s)	Bolivian	Bol.
Bophuthatswana	Tswana	Tswana	Boph.
Botswana	Botswana plural: Batswana	Botswanan	Bots.
Brazil	Brazilian(s)	Brazilian	Braz.
Brunei	Bruneian(s)	Brunei	Bru.
Bulgaria	Bulgarian(s)	Bulgarian	Bulg.
Burkina Faso	Burkinabe	Burkinabe	Burk.
Burundi	Burundian(s)	Burundian	Burundi
Cambodia	Cambodian(s)	Cambodian	Camb.
Cameroon	Cameroonian(s)	Cameroonian	Camr.
Canada	Canadian(s)	Canadian	Can.
Cape Verde	Cape Verdian(s)	Cape Verdian	C.V.
Cayman Islands	Caymanian(s)	Caymanian	Cay. Is.
Central African Republic	Central African(s)	Central African	C.A.R.
Chad	Chadian(s)	Chadian	Chad
Chile	Chilean(s)	Chilean	Chile
China	Chinese	Chinese	China
Ciskei	Ciskeian(s)	Ciskeian	Cisk.
Colombia	Colombian(s)	Colombian	Col.
Comoros	Comoro(s)	Comorian	Com.

N

Region	Resident	Adjective	Abbreviation
Congo	Congolese	Congolese	Congo
Costa Rica	Costa Rican(s)	Costa Rican	C.R.
Croatia	Croat(s), Croatian(s)	Croatian	Croat.
Cuba	Cuban(s)	Cuban	Cuba
Cyprus	Cypriot(s)	Cypriot	Cyprus
Czech Republic	Czech(s)	Czech	Czech.
Denmark	Dane(s)	Danish	Den.
Djibouti	Djiboutian(s)	Djiboutian	Djib.
Dominica	Dominican(s)	Dominican	Dmica.
Dominican Republic	Dominican(s)	Dominican	Dom. Rep.
Ecuador	Ecuadoran(s)	Ecuadoran	Ecua.
Egypt	Egyptian(s)	Egyptian	Egypt
El Salvador	Salvadoran(s)	Salvadoran	El Salv.
Equatorial Guinea	Equatorial Guinean(s)	Equatorial Guinean	Eq. Guin.
Eritrea	Eritrean(s)	Eritrean	Erit.
Estonia	Estonian(s)	Estonian	Est.
Ethiopia	Ethiopian(s)	Ethiopian	Eth.
Falkland Islands	Falkland Islander(s)	Falkland Island	Falk. Is.
Fiji	Fijian(s)	Fijian	Fiji
Finland	Finn(s)	Finnish	Fin.
France	the French, Frenchman(men, woman, women)	French	France
Gabon	Gabonese	Gabonese	Gabon
Gambia	Gambian(s)	Gambian	Gam.
Georgia	Georgian(s)	Georgian	Geor.
Germany	German(s)	German	Germ.
Ghana	Ghanaian(s)	Ghanaian	Ghana
Great Britain	Briton(s), British	Britain, British	G.B.
Greece	Greek(s)	Greek	Gr.
Grenada	Grenadian(s)	Grenadian	Grenada
Guatemala	Guatemalan(s)	Guatemalan	Guat.
Guinea	Guinean(s)	Guinean	Guinea
Guinea-Bissau	Guinean(s)	Guinean	Guin.-Biss.
Guyana	Guyanese	Guyanese	Guy.
Haiti	Haitian(s)	Haitian	Haiti
Honduras	Honduran(s)	Honduran	Hond.
Hong Kong	Hong Kongese, Hong Kongian(s)	Hong Kong	H.K.
Hungary	Hungarian(s)	Hungarian	Hung.
Iceland	Icelander(s)	Icelandic	Ice.
India	Indian(s)	Indian	India
Indochina	Indochinese	Indochinese	Indochina
Indonesia	Indonesian(s)	Indonesian	Indon.

Region	Resident	Adjective	Abbreviation
Iran	Iranian(s)	Iranian	Iran
Iraq	Iraqi(s)	Iraqi	Iraq
Ireland	the Irish, Irishman (men, woman, women)	Irish	Ire.
Isle of Man	Manxman(men, woman, women), the Manx, Manx resident	Manx	Manx
Israel	Israeli(s)	Israeli	Isr.
Italy	Italian(s)	Italian	It.
Ivory Coast	Ivoirian(s)	Ivoirian	Iv. Cst.
Jamaica	Jamaican(s)	Jamaican	Jam.
Japan	Japanese	Japanese	Jap.
Jordan	Jordanian(s)	Jordanian	Jor.
Kashmir	Kashmiri(s)	Kashmiri	Kash.
Kazakhstan	Kazakh(s)	Kazakh	Kaz.
Kenya	Kenyan(s)	Kenyan	Ken.
Kirgizstan	Kirgiz	Kirgizian	Kirg.
Kiribati	Kiribatian(s)	Kiribatian	Kirib.
Kuwait	Kuwaiti(s)	Kuwaiti	Kuw.
Laos	Lao or Laotian(s)	Laotian or Lao	Laos
Latvia	Latvian(s)	Latvian	Lat.
Lebanon	Lebanese	Lebanese	Leb.
Lesotho	Mosotho plural: Basotho	Basotho	Lesotho
Liberia	Liberian(s)	Liberian	Liberia
Libya	Libyan(s)	Libyan	Lib.
Liechtenstein	Liechtensteiner(s)	Liechtenstein	Liech.
Lithuania	Lithuanian(s)	Lithuanian	Lith.
Luxembourg	Luxembourger(s)	Luxembourg	Lux.
Macao	Macaoan(s)	Macaoan	Mac.
Macedonia	Macedonian(s)	Macedonian	Mace.
Madagascar	Malagasy	Malagasy or Madagascan	Madag.
Malawi	Malawian(s)	Malawian	Malawi
Malaysia	Malaysian(s)	Malaysian	Malay., Mal.
Maldives	Maldivian(s)	Maldivian	Mald.
Mali	Malian(s)	Malian	Mali
Malta	Maltese	Maltese	Malta
Marshall Islands	Marshallese	Marshallese	Mrsh. Is.
Mauritania	Mauritanian(s)	Mauritanian	Mauritania
Mauritius	Mauritian(s)	Mauritian	Mauritius
Mexico	Mexican(s)	Mexican	Mex.
Micronesia	Micronesian(s)	Micronesian	Micro.
Moldova	Moldovan(s)	Moldovan	Mold.

Region	Resident	Adjective	Abbreviation
Monaco	Monacan(s)	Monacan	Mon.
Mongolia	Mongol(s)	Mongolian	Mong.
Morocco	Moroccan(s)	Moroccan	Mor.
Mozambique	Mozambican(s)	Mozambican	Moz.
Myanmar	Myanmarese or Burmese	Myanmar	Myan.
Namibia	Namibian(s)	Namibian	Nam.
Nauru	Nauruan(s)	Nauruan	Nauru
Nepal	Nepalese	Nepalese	Nepal
Netherlands	Netherlander(s), Dutchman(men, woman, women), the Dutch, Hollanders	Netherlandish, Dutch, Netherlands	Neth.
New Zealand	New Zealander(s)	New Zealand	N.Z.
Nicaragua	Nicaraguan(s)	Nicaraguan	Nicar.
Niger	Nigerois	Niger	Niger
Nigeria	Nigerian(s)	Nigerian	Nigeria
North Korea	North Korean(s)	North Korean	N. Kor.
Norway	Norwegian(s)	Norwegian	Nor.
Oman	Omani(s)	Oman, Omani	Oman
Pakistan	Pakistani(s)	Pakistani	Pak.
Palestine	Palestinian(s)	Palestinian	Pal.
Panama	Panamanian(s)	Panamanian	Pan.
Papua New Guinea	Papua New Guinean(s)	Papua New Guinean	Pap. N. Gn.
Paraguay	Paraguayan(s)	Paraguayan	Para.
Peru	Peruvian(s)	Peruvian	Peru
Philippines	Filipino(s)	Philippine	Phil.
Poland	Pole(s)	Polish	Pol.
Portugal	Portuguese	Portuguese	Port.
Puerto Rico	Puerto Rican(s)	Puerto Rican	P.R.
Qatar	Qatari(s)	Qatari	Qatar
Réunion	Réunionese	Réunionese	Réun.
Romania	Romanian(s)	Romanian	Rom.
Russia	Russian(s)	Russian	Russ.
Rwanda	Rwandan(s)	Rwandan	Rwanda
St. Christopher and Nevis (often called St. Kitts-Nevis)	Kittitian(s), Nevisian(s)	Kittsian, Nevisian	St. Kt.-Nev.
St. Lucia	St. Lucian(s)	St. Lucian	St. Luc.
San Marino	Sanmarinese	Sanmarinese	S. Mar.
São Tomé and Príncipe	São Toméan(s)	São Toméan	S. Tm. Prn.
Saudi Arabia	Saudi(s)	Saudi Arabian, Saudi	Saudi Ar.

Region	Resident	Adjective	Abbreviation
Scotland	Scot(s), Scotsman (men, woman, women)	Scottish	Scot.
Senegal	Senegalese	Senegalese	Senegal
Seychelles	Seychellois	Seychelles	Seych.
Sierra Leone	Sierra Leonean(s)	Sierra Leonean	S. Leone
Singapore	Singaporean(s)	Singaporean	Sing.
Slovakia	Slovak(s)	Slovak	Slvk.
Slovenia	Slovene(s) or Slovene	Slovenian	Slvn.
Solomon Islands	Solomon Islander(s)	Solomon Islander	Sol. Is.
Somalia	Somali(s)	Somali	Som.
South Africa	South African(s)	South African	S. Af.
South Korea	South Korean(s)	South Korean	S. Kor.
Spain	Spaniard(s)	Spanish	Sp.
Sri Lanka	Sri Lankan(s)	Sri Lankan	Sri Lan.
Sudan	Sudanese	Sudanese	Sud.
Suriname	Surinamese	Surinamese	Sur.
Swaziland	Swazi(s)	Swaziland	Swaz.
Sweden	Swede(s)	Swedish	Sw.
Switzerland	Swiss	Swiss	Switz.
Syria	Syrian(s)	Syrian	Syr.
Taiwan	Taiwanese	Taiwanese	Taiwan
Tajikistan	Tajik(s)	Tajik	Taj.
Tanzania	Tanzanian(s)	Tanzanian	Tanz., Tan.
Thailand	Thai(s)	Thai	Thai.
Togo	Togolese	Togolese	Togo
Tonga	Tongan(s)	Tongan	Tonga
Transkei	Transkeian(s)	Transkeian	Trans.
Trieste	Triestino(s)	Triestine	Triest.
Trinidad and Tobago	Trinidadian(s) for inhabitants generally; Tobagan(s)	Trinidadian, Tobagan	Trin. & Tob.
Tunisia	Tunisian(s)	Tunisian	Tun.
Turkey	Turk(s)	Turkish	Turk.
Turkmenistan	Turkman(men)	Turkmenian	Turkm.
Tuvalu	Tuvaluan(s)	Tuvaluan	Tuv.
Uganda	Ugandan(s)	Ugandan	Uga., Ug.
Ukraine	Ukrainian(s)	Ukrainian	Ukr.

N

Region	Resident	Adjective	Abbreviation
United Arab Emirates Abu Dhabi Ajman Dubai Fujairah Ras al-Khaimah Sharjah Umm al-Qaiwain	Resident of United Arab Emirates or resident of individual state	United Arab Emirate	U.A.E.
Uruguay	Uruguayan(s)	Uruguayan	Uru.
Uzbekistan	Uzbek(s)	Uzbek	Uz.
Vanuatu	Vanuatuan(s)	Vanuatuan	Van.
Venda	Venda(s)	Venda	Ven.
Venezuela	Venezuelan(s)	Venezuelan	Venez.
Vietnam	Vietnamese	Vietnamese	Viet.
Virgin Islands	Resident of Virgin Islands	Virgin Island	V.I.
Wales	Welshman(men, woman, women), the Welsh	Welsh	Wales
Western Sahara	Western Saharan(s)	Western Saharan	W. Sahara
Western Samoa	Western Samoan(s)	Western Samoan	W. Samoa
Yemen	Yemeni(s)	Yemeni	Yemen
Yugoslavia	Yugoslav(s)	Yugoslav	Yug.
Zaire	Zairian(s)	Zairian	Zaire
Zambia	Zambian(s)	Zambian	Zam.
Zimbabwe	Zimbabwean(s)	Zimbabwean	Zim.

native American. A person born in the United States.

Native American. Use for references to American Indians only when it is the expressed preference of the organization or individual involved. Otherwise, use *American Indian, Indian* or the name of the specific tribe.

NATO (North Atlantic Treaty Organization). The abbreviation may be used in a tight lead, but the name should be spelled out as soon as possible in the story.

NATO commands and titles. A typical command: *Allied Forces Southern Europe. Supreme Allied Commander Europe* is an official title, but it would generally be better to use, for example, *Gen. William Aument, supreme allied commander for Europe,* or *General Aument, the NATO commander for Europe*.

naval. Capitalize when part of a name; lowercase otherwise: *Jacksonville Naval Air Station (the naval air station, the naval station), a naval officer*.

Naval Reserve. *the Reserve, Reserve duty, the Reserves,* but *reserves, reservists,* when referring to individual members.

Navy. Capitalize when referring to a particular country's organization: *the U.S. Navy (the Navy, a Navy destroyer), the British Navy (the Navy), Navy Lt. Fred Arble, the U.S. and British navies, a navy.*

NCO (NCOs). Acceptable on second reference to noncommissioned officer(s).

near( ). *a near antique, nearby, a near catastrophe, near miss, nearsighted, near beer, near silk,* but *a nearly perfect circle*.

Near East is a dated term and should be avoided. However, it may be used in historical or archaeological references to the countries near the eastern end of the Mediterranean Sea, including North Africa and the Balkans, specifically the area formerly controlled by the Ottoman Empire. See Middle East.

Nebraska (Neb., NE in addresses)

Nebraskan

Negro(es). Some individuals use the word and some object. Do not use for an individual unless you know it is acceptable. See racial designations.

neo( ). Write combinations solid except before an *o* or a capitalization.

Nevada (Nev., NV in addresses)

Nevadan

New Brunswick. Abbreviate, *N.B.,* only in charts, maps and tables.

New Brunswicker

New England states. See political regions.

newfound

Newfoundland. Abbreviate, *Nfld.,* only in charts, maps and tables.

Newfoundlander

New Hampshire (N.H., NH in addresses)

New Hampshirite

New Jersey (N.J., NJ in addresses)

New Jerseyite

New Mexican

New Mexico (N.M., NM in addresses)

newspapers. Italicize names. Capitalize and italicize *the* only when it is part of the paper's name and when you use the entire name, as in photo credits and formal lists: ***THE NEW YORK TIMES*** (as a photo credit), but *the* ***New York Times, the Times*** (in body type). Italicize the name of the city, locality or country only when it is part of the paper's name: *the* ***Alamogordo Daily News,*** but *the Gonzales* ***Daily Inquirer***. If the locale is not part of the official name, it may be inserted parenthetically: ***THE*** *(BALTIMORE)* ***SUN*** (in a credit), *the Baltimore* ***Sun*** (in body type). A reliable source for newspaper names is the Editor & Publisher International Year Book. See magazines, titles of works.

New World

new world order

New Year's Day

New York (N.Y., NY in addresses). When there is confusion as to whether the city or state is meant, write *New York State* or *New York City*.

New Yorker

nicknames. Use quotes the first time a nickname appears in a given article: *Eric "Slowhand" Clapton*. If for some reason a person with a very familiar nickname appears for the first time with the nickname only, quotes need not be used: *Ted Kennedy, Mack McLarty*. Do not quote nicknames on subsequent use unless there is danger of offense or confusion. Do not create nicknames simply to accommodate headline sizes, to affect a breezy style or to belittle someone. Do not coin or use nicknames or appellations regarded as pejorative, such as *Moonie* or *pro-lifer*.

no. Capitalize if it is in quotes; lowercase if not: *She said "No." She said no*.

No. Use for *number* in such expressions as *the nation's No. 1 volleyball scorer; No. 2; Nos. 1 and 2; She was No. 1; He was the No. 2 draft pick*.

Nobel. *Nobel Peace Prize (the peace prize, a Nobel, the Nobel Prize in literature, a Nobel Prize, Nobel Peace Prizes, Nobel Prizes, Nobels)*.

nobility. Capitalize titles before names and in such forms as *Earl of Avon;* lowercase otherwise: *Baron Bruno Morawski of Sherwood (Baron Morawski, Morawski, the baron); Carl Budnit, Earl of Avon (Budnit, the earl); Countess Carol von Wimpling (Countess von Wimpling, von Wimpling, the countess); Steven, Duke of Dundalk (Duke Steven, Steven, the duke); Sir Bruce Gathrie, Bart. (Gathrie, Sir Bruce, the baronet)*. See Your Honor.

non( ). Write solid except before a capitalization or in confusing combinations: *nonstop, nonnuclear, non-Euclidean, non-oil, non-community-property states*.

none. When *none* precedes a prepositional phrase with a singular object, it always takes a singular verb (*None of the task is finished*). However, in other situations, the choice between singular and plural is not so clear. In general, use a singular verb when *none* means *not a single one (None of the candidates has a discernible platform)*, a plural verb when it means *not any (None of the boys drive foreign cars)*.

no-no. Plural: *no-nos*.

nor. See or.

north, northern. See compass directions.

North Carolina (N.C., NC in addresses)

North Carolinian

North Dakota (N.D., ND in addresses)

North Dakotan

Northwest Territories. Abbreviate, *N.W.T.,* only in charts, maps and tables.

nose to nose. *They stood nose to nose; a nose-to-nose confrontation*.

Nov. See dates, months.

Nova Scotia. Abbreviate, *N.S.,* only in charts, maps and tables.

Nova Scotian

nuclear age

nuclear power plant

number. *a number are; the number is*. See No.

numbered titles. Capitalize as in *Article I (the article)*.

numbers. In general, spell out cardinal and ordinal numbers below 10. Use figures for numbers 10 and up, unless they begin a sentence: *nine salesmen; the eighth door; 10 hammers; the 10th year; 11th-hour reprieve; Twenty-eight years separated the events; The car has six cylinders,* but *a V-6 engine*. Spell out a number after a colon if what follows the colon is a complete sentence: *Result of his speech: Forty million voters switched.*

Switched by his speech: 40 million voters.

EXCEPTIONS. The following numbers should be in figures even when they are less than 10: scores; vote tabulations; ratios; percent and percentages; types of stocks and bonds; time of day and dates; weights; measures; ages of animate objects; military units; when a fraction is added to a number; when using millions, billions, etc.: *They won by 5 runs; The score was 3-2; a 74-to-3 vote; a 5-to-1 ratio; 3 percent; 6 percentage points; seven 6s; 5 o'clock; June 4; 2 pounds; 5 feet; 8-year-old girl; 1st Army; 2½ years; 4 billion fish.*

BUTTING NUMBERS that are normally written in figures may be spelled out if confusion might result otherwise: *She filled 48 eight-ounce glasses.*

DIVIDING BETWEEN LINES. Do not divide a figure at the end of a line if there is any alternative, even rewriting. If a split is unavoidable, it should come after a comma:

350,437,-

402

MILITARY. Use figures for numerical designations of military units: *6th Fleet, 45th Division,* but use roman numerals for Army corps: *VII Corps.*

PLURALS OF NUMBERS. Form plurals by adding s: *B-52s, 1940s, the '30s.*

ROMAN NUMERALS. Use them to designate monarchs, popes, sequential personal names, ships, automobiles and wars: *King George III, Pope John Paul II, Kyle Morris II, the Laughing Lass III, a Lincoln Mark IV, World War I.* When quoting a document that uses roman numerals, keep them roman:

I. Be there.

II. Be on time.

III. Stay late.

SERIES. Whenever numbers are clustered in a series, paragraph or entire article or when related numbers appear repeatedly in an article, figures may be used throughout to facilitate comparison: She bought 7 shares of AT&T, 3 of GM and 20 of United Aircraft.

CASUAL EXPRESSIONS. Spell out numbers in figurative expressions: *I must have told him a thousand times.*

NEGATIVES. Use an en dash or *minus: –15°F; The temperature hit minus 15 degrees Celsius.* **See ages, fractions, headlines, lists, time, weights and measures.**

'Searching for photos at a newsmagazine means I have to work quickly and be willing to shift directions as the news changes. It's exciting and challenging.'

MARILYN O'BRIEN
PHOTO EDITOR

obscenity, profanity, vulgarity. Do not use such material except in quotes and even then never gratuitously or incidentally. When use of such terms is considered essential to a story, get the approval of top editors.

LEVELS OF EXPLICITNESS. If the importance of using a suspect term overrides the offense it may give, use it: *Senator Smarsky said, "Once you're on the president's shit list, you're through."*

If the actual term need not be used but we want to convey its nature explicitly, do so by using an initial letter and hyphens: *"Once you're on the president's s--- list."*

If neither the word nor its nature is important to the story but an explanation is needed, use a bracketed editor's note: *"Once you're on the president's [enemies] list."*

If the word, its nature and its meaning are deemed unnecessary to the story, replace the offensive term with an ellipsis: *"Once you're on the president's . . . list."*

occupations. Lowercase: *electrical engineer Jason Watson,* but *First Engineer Jason Watson* (a title). See titles of persons.

Oct. See dates, months.

off base. *He was off base,* but *an off-base remark.*

off hours. *skiing during her off hours,* but *an off-hours respite.*

office. Capitalize in a name; lowercase otherwise: *Office of Management and Budget (the budget office, the office), the U.S. attorney's office (the office).*

off-limits

off-peak (adjective)

Ohio (OH in addresses; otherwise do not abbreviate)

Ohioan

OK. *OK'd, OK'ing, OK's* (for verb), *OKs* (for plural noun). *A-OK*. Do not use *okay*.

Oklahoma (Okla., OK in addresses)

Oklahoman

old-boy network

old guard. Lowercase when it means any group that has long defended a cause. Capitalize when it refers to Napoleon's Imperial Guard.

Old World

Olympic Games. *Summer Olympic Games, Summer Olympics, the Olympics, summer games, the games, Olympic-size pool.*

once( ). Do not use a hyphen in such combinations as *once popular method*.

one out of . . . Such expressions take a singular verb: *One out of 10 doctors takes a holistic approach,* but *Two in five doctors favor aspirin.* See ratios.

one person, one vote, but *one-person–one-vote election*

onetime (meaning former), *one-time* (meaning happening once)

online. Write solid when referring to computer connections: *Mabel created an online news service. Melissa went online to contact the users' bulletin board.*

only. Take care, because its placement in a sentence can alter the meaning entirely, as the examples show. Generally, *only* should be as close as possible to the word it modifies:
Only I pushed the new car yesterday.
I only pushed the new car yesterday.
I pushed only the new car yesterday.
I pushed the only new car yesterday.

I pushed the new car only yesterday.
I pushed the new car yesterday only.

on stream (adverb), *on-stream* (adjective)

Ontarian. Resident of Ontario.

Ontario. Abbreviate, *Ont.,* only in charts, maps and tables.

onto. To a position on: *He climbed onto a table,* but *The mayor held on to her office. Jones moved on to Chicago.*

OPEC. Acceptable on second reference to the Organization of Petroleum Exporting Countries.

op-ed. Acceptable for opposite-editorial when the meaning is clear.

operas, names of. Follow the opera's capitalization and italicize: ***Tristram und Isolde.*** See titles of works.

OPI. overall-performance index.

or. In sentences using *or* and *nor,* the verb must agree with the noun closest to it: *Neither the banks nor the government is going to back down.*

oral/verbal. Oral refers to what is spoken; verbal refers to what is conveyed in words, either written or spoken.

ordinal numbers. In general, use figures for *10th* and over. See numbers.

O

Oregon (Ore., OR in addresses)

Oregonian

Oriental. *Asian* is generally preferred for references to people.

(-)oriented. *a worker-oriented revolt,* but *The revolt was worker oriented.*

ostmark. Lowercase references to the former East German currency.

ounce(s). Abbreviate, *oz.,* only in charts, maps and tables.

our, ours. See we.

out( ). Generally solid except before capitalization: *outgrow, out-Herod,* but *out-group, out-migrant, out-of-doors, out-of-pocket expenses.*

over. It may be used when dealing with money, volume and ages: *The price was over $5,000. She loaded over 16 tons of grain. Everyone in the group was over 70.* But, to avoid confusion, use *more than* when dealing with other numbers: *The judge charged more than 15 officers.*

over( ). Combines solid except before capitalization.

P

'Stylebooks are useful–to teach writers how to occasionally break the rules. Raymond Chandler had it right: "When I split an infinitive, damn it, I split it so it stays split." '

JAMES POPKIN
SENIOR EDITOR

Pacific Rim, *rim nations*

Pacific states. California, Oregon, Washington and sometimes Alaska and Hawaii. See political regions.

pact. Capitalize as part of an official name; lowercase otherwise: *Warsaw Pact (the pact)*.

page. Capitalize with a number or letter: *Page 13*. Abbreviations, *p., pp.,* are acceptable in charts and tables. See reference notes.

paintings. See titles of works.

palate/palette/pallet. The palate is the roof of the mouth; a palette is a paint-mixing board; a pallet is a storage platform or a bed.

paligarch(s), paligarchy. Acceptable for references to a government run by a network of friends when the context makes the meaning clear.

pan(-). Combinations with lowercase words are usually written solid and lowercase: *panchromatic, pandemic*. Combinations with capitalized words are usually capitalized and hyphenated: *Pan-Germanic, Pan-American,* but *Pan American World Airways, Panhellenic*.

Panama Canal, *the canal*

Panama Canal treaties consist of the Panama Canal Treaty and the Treaty Concerning the Permanent Neutrality and Operation of the Panama Canal.

papacy

papal

paper(-). Combinations not in the dictionary usually should be two words when used as a noun, hyphenated when used as an adjective.

Pap test, *Pap smear*

parallel. Use figures and lowercase: *46th parallel.*

parallel construction. Avoid inconsistent construction, which jars and confuses the reader.
Incorrect: *Drinking late at night can cause belligerency, exhaustion, indigestion and increase absenteeism.*
Correct: *Drinking late at night can cause belligerency, exhaustion and indigestion and increase absenteeism.*
Better: *Drinking late at night can cause belligerency, exhaustion and indigestion. It also increases absenteeism.*
Incorrect: *Birkner cited three reasons for buying municipal bonds:*
Long-run stability
Tax-free status
They give the holder a stake in the community.
Two of these points are things, the third is a statement. They do not fit together in a package, which makes the combination difficult to read and understand.

parentheses. Use parentheses to enclose proper-noun identifiers, certain interpolations and reference notes: ***The** (Junction City, Kan.) **Daily Union,*** but *the Rehoboth Beach, Del., tournament. The tusk sold for 15 kwacha (about $38). Fifty percent of the tenants objected (box on Page 52).* For explanatory insertions, commas and dashes are less abrupt and are usually preferred to parentheses. Use brackets for editorial interpolations in quotes and for parenthetical matter within parentheses: *He said "I will fight [the budget resolution] to the end"; She approached the first senator (Hubert Shawker [left]) with the information*. Put periods outside a parenthesis at the end of a sentence if the inserted matter is part of a larger sentence, inside if the matter stands independently: *Hughlett addressed the motorcyclists (text on Page 77). Susannah was the fourth winner from her family. (A detailed list appears on Page 83.)* Put caption directions in parentheses: *An undercover FBI agent (left) confronts the suspect.* **See phonetic spelling, reference notes.**

parliament. Capitalize when it is the actual name or the translated equivalent of a national legislative body; lowercase when it is not the actual name: *British Parliament (Parliament), the Diet (Japan's parliament)*. A good guide to such names is the annual Political Handbook of the World.

parole/probation. Parole is the release on condition of good behavior of a prisoner whose sentence has not expired; probation is the suspension of a sentence of a person convicted but not yet imprisoned.

particles. When affixed to foreign names, *da, de, della, des, do, du, l', la, ten, ter, van* and *von* are usually kept on second reference. Do so unless you know that the individual customarily drops the particle. Keeping it is seldom incorrect in modern names. A particle repeated in a foreign surname standing alone should be capitalized or lowercased as it appears in the full name, unless it starts a sentence, when it should always be capitalized: *Charles de Gaulle (de Gaulle), Ferdinand de Lesseps (de Lesseps), François de La Gorce (La Gorce),* but *Alexis de Tocqueville (Tocqueville)*.

HISTORIC NAMES should be used in their familiar forms for the sake of recognition: *Wolfgang von Goethe (Goethe), Hernando De Soto (De Soto), Vincent van Gogh (van Gogh), Tomás de Torquemada (Torquemada)*.

FOREIGN-ORIGIN NAMES. Particles are likely to be capitalized in anglicized names of foreign origin, but this is not always the case. On subsequent reference, the particle usually is capitalized or lowercased as in the full name: *Paul de Kruif (a de Kruif book), Lee De Forest (the De Forest genius), James A. Van Allen (the Van Allen belt)*.

part-time (adjective), but *working part time*

part-timer

party. Capitalize in the name of a political group; lowercase alone: *Republican Party, Communist Party (the party), the Democratic and Republican parties, Greens Party*. Capitalize nouns and adjectives referring to membership in parties: *Communist, Conservative, Republican, Green, Socialist, Laborite, Liberal, Monarchist, Know-Nothing, Nazism, Nazi*.

party designation. Avoid the parenthetical form *(D-Md.)* in favor of such constructions as *Sen. Barbara Mikulski, a Maryland Democrat. Democratic Sen. Barbara Mikulski of Maryland. Sen. Barbara Mikulski arrived. The Maryland Democrat voted yes. Sen. Barbara Mikulski headed the Maryland Democratic congressional caucus. The Democratic senators met. Maryland's Barbara Mikulski spoke.*

passenger-mile

passive voice. See active voice.

Passover

pastor. See entries under specific church names.

pay TV (noun), *pay-TV* (adjective)

PC. Acceptable for personal computer, politically correct and political correctness on second reference when the meaning is clear.

PCP. Acceptable for the psychedelic drug phencyclidine on second reference.

PDT. See time zones.

peacekeeper, *peacekeeping*

peacemaker, *peacemaking*

pedal/peddle. To pedal is to propel, as on a bicycle; to peddle is to try to sell.

peninsula. Capitalize when part of a name; lowercase otherwise: *the Iberian Peninsula* (Peninsula is part of the name); *the Italian peninsula* (peninsula is not part of the name).

Pennsylvania (Pa., PA in addresses)

Pennsylvanian

P/E ratio. Acceptable on second reference to *price-earnings ratio*.

per capita. Do not hyphenate.

percent. Use figures except when the number begins a sentence. The % symbol may be used in tabular matter, headlines and boxes: *Interest was 3 percent. Prices posted an 8 percent increase. Unemployment fell only one half of 1 percent. Eighty-one percent of those replying favored McClinton.* Avoid redundancies in data lists (*Percent of Americans who diet regularly: 32%*) by using words like *proportion, rate, ratio, share* and *part* instead of *percent: Proportion of Americans who diet regularly: 32%* or *Americans who diet regularly: 32%*.
SUBJECT-VERB AGREEMENT. The verb number depends on the object of the preposition: *10 percent of the girls were; 10 percent of the bus was*.

percentage. There is little need for this word aside from its use in "percentage point" (*mortgage interest rates rose 2 percentage points*), in such colloquial expressions as *there's no percentage in taking on a squadron of SEALs* and in rare references to the product of a percent computation. For example, in the equation "50 percent of 60 equals 30," *50* is the percent (***not*** the percentage), *60* is the base and *30* is the percentage.

percentage point. If a rate rises from 5 percent to 6 percent, that's an increase of 1 percentage point or 1 point, not 1 percent. As a share, the increase is 20 percent.

perestroika. Russian for "restructuring." Italicize.

period. Use for declarative sentences (*I am well.*), mildly imperative sentences (*Count me out.*), rhetorical questions posed as suggestions (*Will you come here.*) and indirect questions (*She wondered why we were here.*). Periods always go inside quotation marks.
TYPOGRAPHY. *Use a period* at the end of: notes and footnotes; sideheads that are incorporated into a line of body type; and captions, liftout quotes and factoids that contain a complete sentence.
Do not use a period at the end of: headlines and decks, even when they are a complete sentence; sideheads that appear on a separate line; table of contents entries; attributions for quotes; credits, bylines and source lines; and captions, liftout quotes and factoids that do not contain a complete sentence.
Situational use. Entries in charts, tables and boxes generally take a period when they contain a complete sentence and do not take a period when they contain only fragments. However, periods may be used with sentence fragments or not used with complete sentences for consistency within a particular chart, table or box. Chatter in charts, tables and boxes takes a period when it is longer than one complete sentence. Labels end with a period when they are a sentence and with a dash, colon, ellipsis points or no punctuation when they are not a sentence. See abbreviations, captions, ellipsis points, initials.

periodicals. See magazines, newspapers, titles of works.

periods. See ages and eras; cultural designations.

( )person. See gender bias.

persuade. See convince, persuade.

petty officer. See military titles.

phase. *Prepare for Phase 1,* but *It was the first phase of the operation.* See faze/phase.

Ph.D. (Ph.D.'s). No space between Ph. and D.

phonetic spelling. *The symphony composer's family name is Gajewski (pronounced guy-ESS-key).*

phosphor(s) (noun). Any of various solid coatings, such as those used in television picture tubes and fluorescent bulbs, that glow when bombarded by electrons or other subatomic particles.

phosphorescence. The emission of light from an electronically excited molecule or compound.

phosphorous (adjective). Of, like or containing the element phosphorus.

phosphorus (noun). A chemical element.

physical appearance. Do not make references to a person's physical characteristics, such as size, weight, color, hairstyle, imperfections and infirmities, unless they are clearly relevant to the story. See fairness.

picket means the same as *picketer,* so use the shorter word.

pill. Lowercase when it is used in reference to birth control pills.

Place. Spell out and capitalize when part of an address. See addresses.

place names. Capitalize recognized names: *the Mall* (in Washington, D.C.), *Lafayette Park, Lafayette and Potomac parks, Union Station, the Blue Room*. See geographic names, geographic terms, locations and the electronic PLACES list.

planes. See aircraft.

planets. See heavenly bodies.

plate. Capitalize with a number or a letter: *Plate 16 (the plate)*.

platform. Lowercase as in *the Democratic platform*.

plays. Capitalize the name as the play does and italicize. See titles of works.

plea bargaining (noun), *plea-bargaining* (adjective)

Pledge of Allegiance, *the pledge*

PLO. Acceptable on second reference to Palestine Liberation Organization.

plurality. See majority.

plurals. CAPITALIZED TERMS. Lowercase the generic word when it is last: *Yale and Harvard universities; Mississippi, Monongahela and Ohio rivers,* but *the Universities of Michigan and California, Departments of State and Transportation*.
FIGURES. Add s: *1940s, T-38s*.
LETTERS. Add s to multiple letters *(ABCs, PACs)*. Add 's to single letters *(A's, p's and q's),* to multiple letters with periods *(Ph.D.'s)* and where confusion might otherwise result *(SOS's)*.

PROPER NAMES. When a name ends in a sibilant, add *es: Joneses, Truaxes, Cashes*. Otherwise, add *s: the two Marys, the two Germanys, Royal Air Force Tornados,* but *the Rockies, the Alleghenies*.
SAME SPELLING. For words whose singular and plural spellings are the same, like *corps* and *deer,* the number is determined by context and the number of the verb.

plus. When *plus* is used as a conjunction, commas are not usually necessary, but sometimes the cadence of a sentence calls for them:
Intelligence plus luck pulled him through.
Intelligence, plus a strong element of luck, won out.
In figures: *50 million plus,* but *50-plus millions*.

p.m. See time.

PO. Acceptable for *post office* in addresses: *PO Box 642*.

podium. See lectern/podium.

poems. Quote titles of short poems. Italicize titles of collections of poetry and long poems published separately. See titles of works, verse.

policy is generally lowercased in names of governmental lines of action, but capitalize the surrounding words if the names are well established: *the Open Door policy, an open-door policy toward Canada, America's Good Neighbor policy, a good-neighbor policy among Caribbean nations, Russia's New Economic Policy* (official name of a regulation), *Jimmy Carter's economic policy*.

policy maker

policy making (noun), *policy-making* (adjective)

political action committee. *PAC* is acceptable on second reference.

politically correct, political correctness. May be abbreviated, *PC,* on second reference when the meaning is clear.

political divisions. Spell out nine and below; use figures for 10 and above: *Fifth Congressional District, the district; 10th Ward, the ward; 16th Precinct, the precinct*.

political movements. Lowercase political movements and beliefs not tied to a particular party as well as references to persons holding such beliefs unless the movements are derived from proper names: *communism, communist* (in a philosophical sense), *Marxism, Marxist, fascism, fascist, democracy, a democracy, conservative thinking, a socialist* (in thought), *socialist tendencies, monarchist rumblings,* but *the Monarchist Party*. See party.

political regions. The following lists may be altered somewhat to suit particular situations, such as when an article is based on a source other than *U.S. News*'s own analysts.

East	**South**	**Midwest**
NEW ENGLAND STATES	DEEP SOUTH	FARM BELT STATES
Connecticut	Alabama	Iowa
Maine	Georgia	Kansas
Massachusetts	Louisiana	Minnesota
New Hampshire	Mississippi	Nebraska
Rhode Island	South Carolina	North Dakota
Vermont	OTHERS	South Dakota
OTHERS	Arkansas	Wisconsin
Delaware	Florida	OTHERS
New Jersey	North Carolina	Illinois
New York	Tennessee	Indiana
Pennsylvania	Texas	Michigan
	Virginia	Ohio
Border	**Mountain**	**Far West**
Kentucky	Arizona	PACIFIC STATES
Maryland	Colorado	California
Missouri	Idaho	Oregon
Oklahoma	Montana	Washington
West Virginia	Nevada	OTHERS
	New Mexico	Alaska
	Utah	Hawaii
	Wyoming	

(The 10 Eastern states are sometimes referred to as the North Atlantic states, Delaware, New Jersey, New York and Pennsylvania as the Middle Atlantic states. All five Far Western states are sometimes referred to as the Pacific states.)

political terms. Do not use quotes for those that have achieved historic significance or familiarity: *New Deal, Bull Moose, Great Society, New Frontier*. But take care to ensure that the terms are understood: *the Bull Moose campaign of Teddy Roosevelt, Lyndon Johnson's Great Society*. Use quotes with the first reference to new, ephemeral or obscure movements or campaign slogans: *"New Federalism," "Prague Spring," the "Free Doobies" movement*. Some such terms should be quoted, lowercase: *"new right."*

politics is usually singular but sometimes plural, depending on the context: *Politics is the art of the possible; Your politics make me sick.*

poll. Capitalize when part of an organization's name; lowercase otherwise: *Gallup Poll, Harris Poll (the poll)*.

pontiff, *a pontiff, the pontiffs*

pope. Capitalize before a name; lowercase otherwise: *Pope John Paul II (the pope, a pope)*.

Portuguese names. According to a Portuguese statement, "Portuguese do about as they please" in the use of their names. Some surnames are single, as in *Luis Martins*. Some are double, as in *Albino Cabral Pessoa*. Double surnames put the mother's name first and the father's second. Thus if one surname is used in subsequent mention of a person, it should be the last surname. Be sure you are referring to a Portuguese, not a Spaniard; Spanish surnames place the mother's last, and it is a faux pas to use the mother's name alone. Most Portuguese repeat only one surname, but a few choose to repeat both if they have two: *Luis Martins (Martins), João Hall Themido (Themido), Roque Felix Dias (Felix Dias)*. In case of doubt, it is safe to repeat both parts of a double surname. A woman's name before marriage follows the same patterns as a man's. But if *Maria Soares* marries *Ruy Cordeiro,* she almost always becomes *Maria Soares Cordeiro, Mrs. Ruy Cordeiro, Cordeiro* or *Mrs. Cordeiro*. In Portugal, custom permits a woman on marrying to retain her maiden name: *Mrs. Maria Soares*.

possessives. See apostrophe.

post(-). Follow the dictionaries (New World, then Third International, then Random House): *postnatal, post-mortem*. For words not listed there and when *post* precedes a capital letter, use a hyphen: *the post-cold-war economy, post-Watergate attitude, post-crash decisions.*

pound(s). Abbreviation, *lb.,* is acceptable in charts, maps and tables. See weights and measures.

pounds per square inch. Abbreviation, *psi,* is acceptable on second reference and in charts, maps and tables.

pre(-). Combines solid except before capitalization or an e or to avoid confusion: *pre-eminence, pre-eminent, pre-existing, pre-judicial* (before a judicial hearing), *prejudicial* (causing prejudice).

precinct. Capitalize in a name; lowercase alone: *Sixth Precinct (the precinct)*.

precise words. See exact words.

prefixes. See hyphen.

premier/première. Premier is a chief official, first in time or foremost; première is a first performance or a first or leading woman performer: *première* ***danseuse***.

premier, prime minister. They have the same meaning in reference to heads of sovereign governments, but nations have traditionally used one word or the other. In general, use *premier* for the heads of government in France and its former colonies, Russia and the nations of Eastern Europe. Use *chancellor* for Germany and Austria. Use *prime minister* for the Commonwealth nations. For which word to use with a specific nation, consult the Political Handbook of the World (CSA Publications).

preposition at the end of a sentence is better than an awkward phrase.

Presbyterian. Presbyterian Church (U.S.A.) is the main body of Presbyterians, organized in 1983 with the merger of the Presbyterian Church in the U.S. (the Southern organization) and the United Presbyterian Church in the U.S.A. (the Northern organization). *First Presbyterian Church (the church); the Rev. Richard Rouse, pastor, First Presbyterian Church (the pastor, Rouse)*. Elders are elected laypersons: *Karen Cleese, an elder of the Presbyterian Church (U.S.A.); Richard Kraft, a ruling elder*. The stated clerk, an elected official and the highest executive in the overall church organization, may be either a layperson or an ordained minister: *Blaine Mueller, stated clerk of the Presbyterian Church (U.S.A.)*. The general assembly, elected each year, is the top policy-making body. Members are called commissioners. The head of the assembly is the moderator, also elected each year. *Mary Jones, a commissioner to the general assembly (Jones); the Rev. Thomas Byers, a commissioner to the general assembly (Byers); Geneva Roberts, moderator of the general assembly*. Geographically, synods are groups of presbyteries. The Synod of the Mid-Atlantic, for instance, covers a large territory that includes the Washington, D.C., area. The head of a synod is called the synod executive. Presbyteries are groups of congregations. The National Capital Presbytery covers the Washington area. Alternative titles for the head of a presbytery are executive presbyter and general presbyter.

presidency

president. Capitalize before a name; lowercase otherwise: *President Abraham Lincoln (President Lincoln, the president, the U.S. president), company President Todd Van (the president)*. The first names of American presidents need not be used on first reference with the title unless confusion would otherwise result.

president, U.S. Because Grover Cleveland was both the 22nd and the 24th president of the United States, Bill Clinton is the 42nd president but the 41st to hold the office.

president-elect. Capitalize before a name; lowercase otherwise: *President-elect Joseph Walsh.*

presidential

president pro tem of the Senate. Capitalize before a name; lowercase otherwise.

priest. See Roman Catholic Church.

Prince Edward Island. Abbreviate, *P.E.I.,* only in charts, maps and tables.

Prince Edward Islander. *Islander* is acceptable on second reference.

prison. See jail.

prizes. Capitalize names, but lowercase awards representing levels of victory in track meets, fairs, etc.: *the Good Conduct Medal (the medal), Legion of Merit, Pulitzer Prize for fiction (Pulitzer Prize), Silver Star, Nobel Prize in literature, Nobel Peace Prize (the peace prize), Purple Heart, Medal of Freedom, Medal of Honor, silver medal in the 100-meter dash, blue ribbon for best yearling bull.* See fellowship, scholarship.

pro(-). Hyphenate made-up combinations: *pro-union, pro-patent.*

probation. See parole/probation.

profanity. See obscenity, profanity, vulgarity.

professor. Abbreviate and capitalize before a full name; spell out and lowercase otherwise: *Prof. Paul Denzer (Professor Denzer; Denzer, an English professor; the professor), law Prof. Albert Bundy,* but *Paul Denzer, Edgar Allan Poe Professor of English*. When qualifying words make a title more a description than a title, the title may be spelled out and lowercased: *European-history professor Jill Lotto.*

programs. See computer programs, names of.

(-)prone. Combinations are usually hyphenated: *accident-prone.*

pronunciation. See accents, phonetic spelling.

( )proof. Write simple combinations solid, even if they are not in the dictionary, but hyphenate complicated inventions: *rainproof, tamperproof,* but *indoctrination-proof.*

property tax (noun), *property-tax* (adjective)

pro rata (adverb and adjective)

province. Capitalize in a name; lowercase otherwise: *La Belle Province de Québec (Quebec province, the province of Quebec, the province, a province).*

pseudo. Use two words for made-up combinations not in the dictionary; hyphenate when such a combination is used as an adjective: *a pseudo antique, pseudo-antique chairs.*

PST. See time zones.

PTA. Acceptable on all references to Parent-Teacher Association when the meaning is clear.

publications. See magazines, newspapers, titles of works.

public-opinion poll

Puerto Rican

Puerto Rico (use PR only in addresses; use P.R. only in maps, charts and tables)

Pulitzer Prize, *Pulitzer Prize for fiction, Pulitzer Prizes, Pulitzers, the prize for fiction*

punctuation. Use the minimum needed to avoid confusion and promote clarity. Punctuation marks generally take the font of the preceding word or character. Exceptions are parentheses, brackets and the commas used after bold lead-ins in columns like "People." See separate entry for each punctuation mark.

'Quality. It's definitely a team effort.'

JIM DEUTSCHLANDER
QUALITY ASSURANCE MANAGER

Quakers. See Friends, Religious Society of.

quarter. Abbreviate, *qtr.* or *q.,* only in charts, maps and tables. Capitalize, *Q.,* in table stubs. See charts and tables.

quarter century

quasi(-). Use two words for combinations before nouns; hyphenate combinations with adjectives: *quasi editor, quasi-official statement.*

Quebec. Abbreviate, *Que.,* only in maps, charts and tables.

Québécois (plural same): A French Canadian in or from Quebec province. Quebecer(s): Anybody in or from Quebec province.

queen. Capitalize before a name; lowercase otherwise. Use roman numerals: *Queen Elizabeth II (the queen).*

question mark. Put inside quotation marks when the question is part of the quote; otherwise put outside: *"Are you going to Malibu?" Rocky asked Dennis. How can you tell if the "time is right"?* See period.

quotation marks. STATEMENTS. Put quotation marks around wording quoted verbatim from an informant, speaker, document, book, magazine article or similar source. Do not place marks around material that has been paraphrased or altered in any other way except by nonsubstantive style changes or by deletions indicated with ellipsis points or by explanatory matter inserted between brackets. Complete texts or lengthy excerpts appearing as separate features or boxes sometimes go without quotation marks, but they must be properly introduced to make their origin clear. Interviews and conversations are not in quotation marks.

TITLES. Set in roman type and put quotation marks around titles of short poems, essays, short stories, articles, pamphlets, booklets, lectures, speeches, dissertations, monographs, theses, reports, chapters, songs, radio and television programs, including made-for-television movies, and headlines. Set in italic type, no quotes, names of books, plays, movies, operas, oratorios and other long musical compositions with distinctive names, ballets, paintings, sculpture, computer programs, collections of poetry and long poems published separately, and periodicals, such as newspapers, magazines and newsletters. Standard reference and religious books, such as dictionaries, encyclopedias, the Bible and the Koran, are roman, no quotes.

PARTIAL SENTENCES beginning a quote may lead directly into a continuation of the quote: *Brown said that the building "is a monstrosity. It should be torn down and replaced."*

PUNCTUATION. Commas and periods always come before a close quote, even if they have nothing to do with the matter quoted: *Senator Wenta said he had not seen "East of Eden," but Morris has seen it twice. Senator Sullivan still votes with Senator Flinchum, even though she has referred to him as a "bunco artist."* Semicolons go outside quotation marks. Colons, exclamation marks and question marks are placed inside quotation marks when part of the quotation; otherwise they are outside: *One question the president kept asking himself: Who were these "cronies"?*

He demanded, "Who are they?"

Hughlett said, "Jail the thieves"; Carson put them away.

Zappardino had this to say about "sly embezzlers": They slink.

YES AND NO. Quote when capitalized; no quotes when lowercase:

I say yes. You say no.

I say "Yes." You say "No."

SINGLE QUOTES. Use single quotes in headlines, decks, stylized liftout quotes and subquotes. Use double quotes in precedes, captions, subheads and body type. All-cap Outlook heads integrated with body type are considered headlines and so take single quotes.

MISCELLANEOUS. Do not quote slang, designations of political faith or names of buildings, homes, ships, boats or planes. **See accents, italics, nicknames, titles of works, ( ) word.**

quotations. We use two main kinds of quotations: (1) Language from printed articles, documents, letters and similar records, including recorded *USN&WR* interviews. (2) Language attributed to others in reporters' memories or notes. These two kinds require a shade of difference in treatment.

WHEN LANGUAGE IS ON RECORD, we make no changes beyond those required by printing style, such as spelling or capitalizing words our way or moving commas from a position after quotation marks to before—and even here, we have to be careful if there is a danger of altering the meaning. If we leave anything out, we must indicate a deletion. To condense or otherwise change a statement so that it sounds better in our context—unless we have the writer's permission—is beyond our province; the only way to make such changes is to paraphrase, outside of quotation marks.

IN QUOTATIONS FROM MEMORY or from notes taken on the scene, it is up to a reporter to tell what the person said, not what the reporter thinks the person meant to say or ought to have said. If the quote does not make sense as spoken, the only solution is to give up the quote or query the person quoted. Details such as punctuation are the duty of the reporter and the editors, who must place commas and periods in such a way as to give the most accurate account of what was spoken.

PRONUNCIATION is largely in the ear of the hearer. It is hard to prove how somebody spoke, and, in any case, doubt always remains as to whose pronunciation is correct. To call attention to pronunciation by misspelling a word is often to ridicule the speaker. Only in a rare case—for instance, in an article about a member of Congress who makes a point of being a personality and when we know it is all right with the person quoted—should we ever stress pronunciation.

A QUOTEE'S GRAMMAR is the quotee's own and should not routinely be cleaned up to meet our own publishing standards. Even a college professor should not be made to talk as if at a lecture. If the professor told us, "I don't know who we ought to hire," we should let the professor say it that way. On the other hand, if the professor said, "Them boys . . . ," and we don't think it was said on purpose, we may judge it best to change it and spare the professor embarrassment.

LIFTOUT QUOTES. When a quotation is pulled from a story and set in large type, put a period at the end if the quote is a complete sentence. When a liftout consisting of words written by us, as in an editorial or a column, varies from the wording in the article itself, drop the quotation marks.

R

'Someone said wars start because diplomats tell lies to journalists, then believe what they read. So our public trust should always include a healthy skepticism and a ravenous appetite for fact and truth.'

MIKE RUBY
CO-EDITOR

racial designations. Do not use racial or ethnic designations unless they are clearly essential to the story. See African-American, Asian, black, Chicano, colored, Hispanic, Latino, Negro.

rack, wrack. As a noun, use *rack* to mean a framework; as a verb, use it to mean to spread out, torture, trouble, torment or score: *The suspect was tortured on the rack. She racked her brain. The suspense was nerve-racking. She racked up 15 straight points.* Use *wrack,* as a noun, to mean ruin or destruction; as a verb, use it to mean to ruin or destroy: *wrack and ruin; The car was wracked up by the train.*

radio. Quote the names of programs.

railroad, railway. Spell out and capitalize as part of a name; lowercase alone. Note that Rail Road is two words in some names.

railroad abbreviations. Use an ampersand, no periods, no spaces: *B&O.*

R&D. Acceptable on second reference to *research and development.*

rank and file, *a rank-and-file decision*

rathole

ratios. Use figures: *She reported that 3 of every 4 Californians support Proposition 19; the ratio was 2 to 1, a 2-to-1 ratio*. But when the first number is spelled out, as at the beginning of a sentence, spell out the second number as well if it is less than 10: *One in three Americans believes Satan is real.*

raw material (noun), *raw-material* (adjective)

re(-). Write solid except before an e or capitalization, or in confusing combinations: *re-cover* (to cover anew), *re-form* (to form again), *re-create* (to create again).

(-)ready. Usually hyphenated in combinations: *battle-ready, combat-ready,* but *combat readiness*.

real estate, *real-estate broker*

Realtor is a trademark. Use only for members of the National Association of Realtors. Generic equivalents are *real-estate broker, real-estate agent, real-estate specialist*.

Red. Do not use as a synonym for Communist. If it appears that way in a quotation or in a historical context, capitalize it.

reference books. Use roman type, no quotes, for titles of well-known standard reference books such as encyclopedias, dictionaries and almanacs: *Encyclopedia Americana,* but ***The Encyclopedia of Beach Volleyball***. See book titles, titles of works.

reference notes. Use parentheses: *(box on Page 80)* or *(box, Page 80)*. Avoid language, like *(see box, Page 80),* that suggests we are ordering readers about.

regiment. Capitalize in a name; lowercase alone: *5th Regiment, 41st Regiment, the regiment*.

regions. See nations and regions; political regions.

Regular Army

reign/rein. Reign is to rule or prevail; rein is to restrain or guide.

religious denominations. Capitalize official and shortened names; lowercase *church* by itself: *The Roman Catholic Church (the Catholic Church, the church), the Episcopal Church (the church)*. See church, denominations and separate entries for particular denominations.

religious personages. Capitalize personages in religious lore and history: *the Baptist, the Blessed Virgin, Buddha, Messiah, Mother of God, the Prophet* (meaning Muhammad), *Queen of Heaven, the Virgin, the Virgin Mary*. See deity.

Religious Society of Friends. See Friends, Religious Society of.

Rep. Abbreviate when used before a complete name as a title (*Rep. Tina Kasparowitz*). Spell out when used with a last name (*Representative Kasparowitz*). Spell out and lowercase otherwise (*the representative*). Avoid using the abbreviation in situations where it might be confused with *Republican*. See congressman.

repetition. Avoid undue repetition of a word or phrase, which can distract readers or turn them off. At the same time, realize that in some situations repetition is acceptable and even desirable or necessary, and beware of avoidance techniques whose cure is worse than the disease.

representative at large. *Rep. at Large Henry Lewis, the representative at large, a representative-at-large election*.

republic. Capitalize when part of a name; lowercase otherwise: *Dominican Republic (the republic), Republic of Namibia, Serbian Socialist Republic,* but *the republic of Serbia*.

Republican. Abbreviate, *Rep.* or *R,* but only in charts, maps and tables and then only when it will not be confused with *representative*.

Republican national chairman. Capitalize before a name; lowercase otherwise: *Republican National Chairman Clyde Backhaus (the Republican national chairman)*.

Republican National Committee. *the committee*.

Republican National Convention. *the national convention, the GOP convention*.

Republican Party. *Republicans, the party, the GOP*.

Reserve(s). Capitalize for a specific military group; lowercase for members. See Army Reserve, Naval Reserve, etc.

Reserve Officers Training Corps (ROTC)

resister/resistor. A resister is one who or that which resists; a resistor is an electrical device.

restrictive clauses. See that, which.

retired. Abbreviate in parentheses when used after a name: *Lt. Gen. Bernard Grady, USA (Ret.); Rear Adm. Doug Yerkes, USN (Ret.)*.

reverend, the (the Rev.). Abbreviate before a full name; spell out otherwise: *the Rev. Willy Wirtz;* on second reference, *Wirtz* or, alternatively in the case of Roman

Catholics and some Episcopalians, *Father (Mother) Wirtz*. Do not use *Reverend, Rev.* or *the Rev.* with the last name only. The *the* may be dropped in headlines, charts, tables and letters-to-the-editor signatures and to follow an individual's preference. Do not use double titles, such as *the Rev. Dr. Arberg*. See titles of persons and entries for specific churches.

revolution. Capitalize historical names: *the French Revolution, the American Revolution*. Capitalize *Revolutionary War* and *the Revolution* when referring to the American Revolution. Lowercase *revolution* standing alone when it refers to something other than the American Revolution. Lowercase plural constructions: *the French and American revolutions*.

revolutions per minute. Abbreviation, *rpm,* is acceptable after first reference.

Rhode Island (R.I., RI in addresses)

Rhode Islander

Rhodes scholar. See scholarship.

riffle/rifle. Riffle is to leaf rapidly through; rifle is to ransack or pillage.

right. Lowercase unless it is part of the official name of a political party: *the right wing of the party, a right-wing caucus*. Don't use *right-winger* except in quoted matter.

right of way, *right-of-way contract*

right-to-life. See abortion-debate terminology.

river. Capitalize as part of a name; lowercase alone: *Red River (the river), the Mississippi and Missouri rivers*.

Road. Spell out and capitalize in an address. See addresses.

rockets. For names not listed here, consult Jane's All the World's Aircraft and Jane's Weapon Systems, but make all figures arabic regardless of Jane's usage.
U.S. ROCKETS and rocket stages generally are known by popular names, which sometimes are followed by numerals that stand for model numbers: *Titan 3, Saturn 5, Minuteman 3, Titan 3D, S-4B* (rocket stage). Submarine-launched missiles are known by their names, sometimes followed by letters and numbers: *Polaris A-2, Poseidon C-3, Polaris A-3, Trident 1*.
RUSSIAN ROCKETS: *SS-4, SS-9, SS-14*. Surface-to-air (antiaircraft) missiles are designated by SA and number: *SA-3*. Most of these missiles have been given names, but they are usually known by letter and number.

role/roll. A role is a part or a character; a roll is a membership list or a bun.

roll call, *roll-call vote*

rollover (noun and adjective)

Roman Catholic Church. *the Catholic Church, St. James's Roman Catholic Church (the church, a Roman Catholic church, a Roman Catholic), the Rev. Xavier Moore, pastor of St. James's Roman Catholic Church (the pastor, Father Moore, the priest, O'Donnell)*. Priest is a proper vocational description for ordained persons from a pastor to and including the pope.
Bishop Xavier Proctor of Atlanta (Bishop Proctor, the bishop, Proctor)
Cardinal Xavier Cook (Cardinal Cook, the cardinal, Cook)
Pope Leo XIII (Pope Leo, Leo, the pope, a pope)
Msgr. Thomas Cox (Monsignor Cox, the monsignor, Cox)
Monsignor is an honorary title conferred by the pope on some priests who are not bishops. Do not use two titles: *the Rev. Msgr. Xavier O'Donnell.*
the Very Rev. and *the Most Rev.* are used in referring to the superiors general of some Roman Catholic orders.
SACRAMENTS of the Roman Catholic Church, some of which are shared by other denominations:
anointing of the sick, essentially the rite formerly called extreme unction. Say "administered last rites" if that is what they were, or "administered the sacrament of anointing" to the person.
baptism
confirmation
Eucharist, eucharistic; Holy Communion, Communion, also in some denominations *the Lord's Supper*
holy orders (ordination ceremonies of the priesthood)
matrimony (the marriage ceremony)
reconciliation (penance)

roman numerals. See numbers.

roman type

room. Capitalize in a name or with a number or a letter: *East Room, the Blue Room, Room 320, Room 3A.*

ROTC. Acceptable on first reference to Reserve Officers Training Corps if context makes the meaning clear.

round. *Round 12, Round 4, 12th round, fourth round, 12th-round knockout.*

route. See highway names.

royalty. Princes and princesses are "royal highnesses"; reigning monarchs are "majesties." Use such terms only when quoting someone.

R.R. Use as an abbreviation for *Railroad* only in charts, maps and tables.

Rt. Rev.

run-up (noun)

Russian. Do not use for references to non-Russian citizens of the former Soviet Union or of the Commonwealth of Independent States. For references to individuals and specific groups, use the applicable national term, such as *Russians, Georgians, Armenians, Ukrainians*.

Russian names. Russian names are transliterated several ways with a variety of results. Follow the spellings of individuals who have made their preferences known, then use the electronic NAMES list, then Webster's New World Dictionary and Webster's Biographical Dictionary. For unfamiliar names, follow these rules of thumb:
Spell names beginning with an e sound *ye*:
Yevgeni, not *Evgeni*
Yecaterina, not *Ecaterina*
But in the interior of a name, do not use the *ye* form:
Dostoevsky, not *Dostoyevsky*
Sergeevich, not *Sergeyevich*
Familiar names that are known to have the *yo* sound for e should be spelled that way:
Pyotr, not *Petr*
Fyodor, not *Fedor*
If in the transliteration that comes to you a name is spelled with an e with umlaut, treat the word as you would if it were spelled with an ordinary *e:*
Pëtr: Pyotr
Zhigalëv: Zhigalev
Use *x,* not *ks*:
Alexei, not *Aleksey*
Alexander, not *Aleksandr*
Use *c,* not *k*:
Victor, not *Viktor*
Use the ending *i* rather than *y, iy, yi, yj, ii, ij* for first and last names:
Dmitri, not *Dmitriy*
Grigori, not *Grigoriy*
Georgi, not *Georgiy*
Yuri, not *Yuriy*
but *Tolstoy* (historical)
Use these endings:
-*sky* (-*ski* is Polish)

-*ov* (-*off* is French)
-*ev* (-*eff* is French)
Use the feminine ending in a last name if the woman has an independent reputation; otherwise keep the masculine ending: *Natalia Makarova,* not *Makarov,* but *Victoria Brezhnev,* not *Brezhneva.*
For the feminine ending in first names, use *ia,* not *iya* or *iia*:
Victoria, not *Victoriya*
Lidia, not *Lidiya*
Maria, not *Marya*
Natalia, not *Nataliya*

Ry. Use as an abbreviation for Railway only in charts, maps and tables.

R

S

'A good proofreader needs an eye for detail, the willingness to take nothing for granted, insatiable curiosity and diplomatic skills.'

JIM SWEENEY
PROOF DESK CHIEF

sacraments. Capitalize Eucharist, Holy Communion, Communion, Lord's Supper. Lowercase anointing of the sick, baptism, confirmation, holy orders, matrimony, sacrament of reconciliation, mass, high mass, low mass, requiem mass.

Saint, Sainte (*St.* and *Ste.*). Use the abbreviations for all saints, geographical names and organizations. Alphabetize as if they were spelled *Saint* and *Sainte*.

Saskatchewan. Abbreviate, *Sask.,* only in charts, maps and tables.

Saskatchewanian

Satan. Capitalize *Devil* when it means Satan, but lowercase *devils, a devil*.

satellites. See space vehicles.

savings and loan association. Use an ampersand in abbreviations and in official names: *S&L, S&Ls, Zappardino Savings & Loan Association, the savings and loan*.

savings bonds, *U.S. savings bonds*

say is the all-purpose neutral verb of attribution. Exercise care when using others, which can carry additional meaning:
state adds formality.

declare and *proclaim* add formality or openness or imply an official announcement.
assert is to say confidently.
allege is to assert, especially without proof.
indicate and *suggest* add a tentative or indirect quality.
maintain implies defensiveness.
claim implies that the writer has reason to disbelieve what was said. A more neutral alternative is *assert*.
note, affirm and *point out* imply that what is said is demonstrably true. Use only when dealing with facts, not opinions, claims or speculation.
disclose and *reveal* imply past concealment.
admit implies shame or confession.
laugh, chuckle, snort, etc., are generally amateurish and should be used sparingly, if at all.

Scandinavian countries. Norway, Sweden and Denmark. Iceland and the Faero Islands are sometimes included, as is Finland, but Finland is related by language to Estonia and Hungary rather than to Scandinavia.

scene. Capitalize with a number; lowercase alone: *Scene 1 (the scene)*.

schedule. Capitalize with a number or a letter; lowercase alone: *Schedule D, Schedule 25 (the schedule)*.

scholar. Lowercase as in *Rhodes scholar*.

scholarship. Capitalize in the name of an award; lowercase alone: *a Rhodes Scholarship (the scholarship, a Rhodes scholar)*.

school. See colleges and universities.

school subjects. Capitalize the names of specific courses and proper nouns; lowercase otherwise: *Literature II, Journalism 202, Latin, Greek, English history, mathematics, calculus*.

scores. Use figures.

S corporation

Scotch (adjective). In general, use *Scotch* when referring to things (*Scotch whisky*), *Scottish* when referring to people (*Scottish voters*).

Scotch whisky, but *whiskey* for generic references. See whiskey.

SEAL (SEALs). Nickname for members of the sea, air and land forces of the Naval Special Warfare Command.

seasons. Lowercase unless they are personified: *spring of 1977, ". . . when Autumn came on in her bright bangles."*

second(s). Abbreviate, *sec.,* only in charts, maps and tables. Spell out below 10; use figures above nine. See numbers.

Second, the. In names, use roman numerals, no commas: *King William II, Frederick Arble II*. Do not use unless an individual is known that way or it is necessary to distinguish one person from another. See numbers.

secretariat

secretary. Capitalize when part of a formal title before a name; lowercase otherwise: *Secretary of State Hubert Shawker (the secretary of state)*.

secretary general. Capitalize before a name; lowercase otherwise: *U.N. Secretary General Kerry Kelly (Secretary General Kelly, the secretary general)*.

section. Capitalize with a number or letter; lowercase otherwise: *Section 2, the second section, the section*.

Security Council (of the United Nations), *the council*

self(-). Hyphenate made-up combinations.

semi( ). Write combinations solid except before a capital letter or an *i*.

semicolon. It is useful where a somewhat more authoritative stop than a comma is needed. Place semicolons outside quotation marks.
IN A COMPOUND SENTENCE, a semicolon can provide a pleasing balance: *Tad played faster; Crystal worked harder.* Semicolons in this type of sentence can add interest and variety to copy. Overuse, however, can produce a formal style that reads like an essay. Avoid merely stringing ideas together with semicolons when their relationship needs more explanation.
DIVISIONS BETWEEN PHRASES that already have commas should be made with semicolons. Use either a comma or a semicolon before the *and* preceding the last item in a series, depending on the complexity: *The trend was strong in Biloxi, Miss.; Richmond, Va., and Rockport, Mass. They chose cattle wrangling and plinking in Wyoming; bird-watching in Canada and Greece; volleyball in Florida; and salmon fishing in Scotland.*

Senate. Capitalize references to the U.S. Senate or to a legislative body of a state or a foreign country if that is the name it uses. Abbreviate, *Sen.,* only in charts, maps and tables.

senator. Capitalize and abbreviate before a full name; spell out with last name only; lowercase otherwise: *Sen. Bruno Moore (Senator Moore, the senator), a senator, two senators*. See party designations.

senatorial

sentence fragments. Favored by automobile-advertisement copywriters, sentence fragments in news copy are almost always too precious. And difficult to understand. Which is why they should be used rarely. If at all.

sentence length. A mixture of short and longer sentences, with a variety of constructions, will help keep the reader alert and interested. Sudden insertion of a short, blunt sentence achieves emphasis. No sentence should be so long that the reader loses track of the beginning before reaching the end; re-examination of an article frequently turns up a sentence or two of this kind. A succession of one-sentence paragraphs, favored by some writers, does not necessarily help clarity; it may have the opposite effect because the reader is left to puzzle out what is related to what and how. Newsmagazine paragraphs should be reasonably short, it is true, but with each paragraph organized around a topic. An exception is a collection of single-sentence paragraphs in a series introduced by a colon or a dash.

Sept. See dates, months.

series. *series E savings bonds, series EE, series H, series HH*.

service. Capitalize in a name; lowercase otherwise: *Internal Revenue Service (the revenue service, the service)*.

set-aside (noun)

set-to (noun)

sexism. See gender bias, he/she, man.

she, her. Do not use for countries, ships, hurricanes or tropical storms.

sheik. Capitalize before a name; lowercase alone.

ships, names of. Capitalize, roman, no quotes. Use *it,* not *she*.

short stories. Quote titles. See titles of works.

[sic]. Confine its use to typographical errors or serious mistakes in usage that we have left in quoted material. Do not use merely to call attention to someone's incorrect grammar. Set it in italics and brackets with no period: *She wrote that her husband "was unphased [**sic**] by the allegations."* See quotations.

( )sick. Usually combines solid: *heartsick*.

sign off (verb), *sign-off* (noun)

signs. In some cases, small caps, with no quotation marks, are appropriate for body-type references to signs and headlines: *Virginia's sign said* WE LUV JOHNNY KAY. When not using small caps, enclose signs and headlines in quotation marks.

six-cylinder. *eight cylinders, sixes, eights, V-8, V-6*.

(-)size. Hyphenate combinations except those with a prefix that normally forms one word: *whale-size, midsize*. Follow the dictionary on spelling: *oversize, middle-sized, undersized*. For words not in the dictionary, use *-size: full-size, family-size*.

size up (verb), *size-up* (noun)

slang, dialect and jargon. Slang and other nonstandard words create an on-the-scene ambience. They sound best in quotations from others, but we can use them to advantage in our own writing if we do it well. The absolute element is clarity to all readers. Nonstandard words are often understood only in certain regions or trades or by limited social, ethnic or age groups. Therefore, if we use such a word we have to make sure, by context or by subtle explanation, that the meaning is plain. Do not use quotation marks around nonstandard words unless the intention is to attribute them to individuals or groups identified or implied in the copy. If we have to apologize for a word, we should not write it. Use Webster's New World Dictionary as a guide to distinguishing nonstandard words by such terms as *slang, colloquial* and *regional*.

Slovak. See **Czech, Czechoslovak**.

small-business man, *small-business woman, small-business executive, small-business investment company*. See **businessman, businesswoman; gender bias**.

S.O.B. (S.O.B.'s). Use only when quoting someone. Don't use when someone in fact said "son of a bitch." See **obscenity, profanity, vulgarity**.

so-called (adjective), *so called* (adverb). Use either quotation marks or *so-called;* don't use both. S

Social Security. Capitalize in reference to the U.S. system; lowercase generic references: *your Social Security number, social security systems in Europe*.

society. Capitalize in a name; lowercase otherwise: *Philadelphia Saving Fund Society (the society), high society*.

someday/some day. Someday means an indefinite time in the future: *I'll see*

Mary Louise someday, but *some day in June, on some day that I'll tell you later.*

someplace/some place. *I left it someplace,* but *He is moving to some place in Arkansas.*

sometime, some time. Adverb (at some time not known or specified): *It will happen sometime.* Adjective (former, occasional): *a sometime co-worker.* But when it means a certain or indefinite period: *It happened some time ago.*

SOS (plural: *SOS's*)

sound bite

source lines. Most charts, maps and tables have source or basic-data lines. Set source lines in caps and lowercase. They are usually introduced by ***USN&WR.*** If more than one source is listed, separate them by commas unless semicolons are necessary for clarity. Federal agencies are designated as U.S. and—an exception to style followed elsewhere—the abbreviations *Dept.* and *Depts.* are used for cabinet agencies. Otherwise, give the complete name of the agency, and avoid abbreviations that would not be used in body copy, except ***USN&WR***. Follow general style for italics, quotation marks and accents:
USN&WR—*Basic data: U.S. Depts. of Labor, Commerce; estimates by* ***USN&WR*** *Research Department*
USN&WR—*Basic data: U.S. Treasury Dept.,* ***National Geographic***
USN&WR—*Basic data: Federal Communications Commission*
Robert Cooke—***USN&WR***
Avoid complete sentences in source lines, and do not use a period at the end.
The Art Department indicates the position of the source line on its layout for the chart or table. Source lines for boxed charts usually run inside the rules or on the color panel that defines the borders of the box. Sometimes the source lines are placed outside the apparent boundaries of charts. The News Desk edits source lines for style and content and checks their position to make sure that each line covers the portion of the chart to which it applies. **See captions.**

sources. Such phrases as *officials said, observers said, experts said* and *a spokesman said* are evasive; they can leave the general reader vaguely unsatisfied and the insider suspecting that the officials are a doorman, the observers are a bartender, the experts are our reporter and the spokesman is the third vice president's secretary. We must get as close as possible to naming real persons while remaining within the source's guidelines for attribution. Sample lines of retreat:
FOR OFFICIALS
Secretary of Agriculture Franklin Farman
a top official in the Department of Agriculture
officials who have studied the agreement
Agriculture officials
federal officials or officials in Washington

FOR OBSERVERS
British Ambassador Monique John
a Western ambassador who is a veteran in the Middle Eastern service
a veteran diplomat
Western diplomats on the scene
old hands in the Middle East
See expert.

south, southern. Capitalize in a name or when designating the southern United States; lowercase when merely indicating a direction: *the South, the Deep South, Southerner, Southern states, South Pole, the Southwest (United States), Southern Hemisphere, South Side* (of Chicago), *southern New Jersey, They headed south.* See compass directions, political regions and the PLACES electronic file.

South Carolina (S.C.; SC in addresses)

South Carolinian

South Dakota (S.D.; SD in addresses)

South Dakotan

Soviet (adjective). Capitalize in references to the former Soviet Union: *Soviet government, Soviet citizens, Soviet cars.*

Soviet (noun). Capitalize in names; lowercase when used alone to refer to governmental bodies: *The village soviet sent its five-year plan to the Supreme Soviet.*

Soviets. Capitalize references to what was the government of the U.S.S.R. and to its people: *In 1990, the Soviets offered tractors for wheat.*

space age. See ages and eras.

space vehicles. Individual U.S. space vehicles and missions use names, frequently with arabic numerals added to show number in a series: *Viking 2, Pioneer 11, GEOS 3* (for Geodynamics Satellite).
RUSSIAN SPACE VEHICLES and missions are generally treated in the same way: *Cosmos 629, Sputnik 1, a sputnik.*
SPACE COMMAND SHIPS, landers, moon cruisers, etc., are referred to by name or description without quotes or italics: *Casper* (orbiting command ship), *Orion* (lander), *Kitty Hawk* (command ship), *Antares* (lander), *space buggy, moon rover, Lunokhod 1, space shuttle Discovery.*
LAUNCH VEHICLES, SPACE PROBES AND SATELLITES are usually referred to by names, with figures or letters: *Intelsat 4, Agena D, Hubble Space Telescope (the space telescope).*

Spanish-language names. The only safe guide to Spanish-language names is the way the individuals use them. Surnames are usually double, the father's (patronymic) first, the mother's (matronymic) last. *Joaquín Prado Fernández* on second reference would be *Prado Fernández* or *Prado,* not *Fernández*. Some double names derive from one person alone when the person has achieved fame. Spain's former prime minister, *Leopoldo Calvo Sotelo,* is a nephew of *José Calvo Sotelo,* whose assassination touched off the Spanish Civil War. He is *Calvo Sotelo* on second reference. Former Mexican President *José López Portillo*'s double surname derives from his grandfather. Sometimes what looks like a double surname is not. *Carlos Andrés Pérez* of Venezuela uses only his patronymic. *Andrés* is a given name. Cuban cabinet minister *Carlos Rafael Rodríguez* (*Rafael* is a given name) does not use his matronymic, probably because it is the same as his patronymic. Sometimes given names are compounds. *María de los Angeles Moreno Uriegas* is *Moreno* on second reference. Sometimes the surname is a compound. Mexican President *Carlos Salinas de Gortari* is usually referred to as *Salinas* on second reference. But former United Nations Secretary General *Javier Pérez de Cuéllar* is *Pérez de Cuéllar* on second reference.
GENERAL RULES
1. Use a name as the individual uses it or as it is used in the local environment.
2. On second reference, use the first surname unless you know that the individual uses both surnames.
3. Avoid using the second surname alone. However, certain well-known individuals with common surnames are referred to by their matronymic. The poet *Federico García Lorca* is called *Lorca* or *García Lorca,* never *García,* which is the Smith of the Spanish language. Some persons with common surnames add the initial of the matronymic: *Enrique González R.* This looks odd and should be used only if there is real doubt about which *González* is meant.
WOMEN'S NAMES. If *María Pérez* marries *José González,* she becomes *María Pérez de González;* on second reference, *González.*

spartan. Lowercase references to people or things characterized by self-discipline, self-denial or frugality (*spartan accommodations*); capitalize references to ancient Sparta (*Spartan politics*).

speaker. Capitalize as a title before a name; lowercase alone: *Speaker of the House Lily Myers (Speaker Myers, the speaker), speakership.*

Specialist. See military titles.

special prosecutor. See independent counsel.

speeches. See titles of works.

spelling. Use the following guides in this order:
1. This stylebook, including the electronic NAMES and PLACES word lists.
2. The preferred entry given in Webster's New World Dictionary, Third College

Edition (Simon & Schuster). The preferred entry is taken to mean the one first mentioned; however, when the dictionary specifies "usually" with an alternative spelling for a particular definition, use that spelling.
3. Webster's Third New International Dictionary (G.&C. Merriam Co.). See geographic names, Russian names, Spanish-language names, etc.

split infinitive. See infinitives.

split-level (noun and adjective)

spokesperson. See gender bias.

sport/sports (adjective). *sports car, sports clothes, sports medicine, sports editor, sports section* but *sport coat, sport fish, sport shirt.*

sputnik. Capitalize only in the name of an individual satellite: *Sputnik 1 (the sputnik, a sputnik)*. See space vehicles.

spymaster

Square. Spell out and capitalize in a name or an address; lowercase alone.

Sr. Do not set off with commas: *H. Ralph Nickerson Sr. came home.*

St. See Saint, Sainte.

stanch/staunch. Stanch means to stop the flow; staunch means steadfast or loyal.

stars. See heavenly bodies.

state. Lowercase when referring to one or more states of the United States: *a state, the state, state Sen. Ashley Jones, the state Capitol.* Capitalize in names: *State Produce Inc., New York State, the Empire State, Washington State, the State of Israel,* but *the state of Washington, the state of Maryland.* When a city and state are used adjectivally in a proper name, put the state in parentheses: *They found the Radford (Va.) University student at home.* Or consider rewriting: *They found the student from Virginia's Radford University at home.* See states.

statehouse. Capitalize references to a specific statehouse: *the Mississippi Statehouse (the Statehouse),* but *the Mississippi and Missouri statehouses.*

state of the art. It means the current level of sophistication. Do not use as a synonym for *high tech* or *fancy.*

State of the Union message, *State of the Union address*

states. When the name of a state appears as part of a complete mailing address, use the Postal Service abbreviation, which is in the second or fifth column below. Otherwise, use the traditional abbreviation listed in the third or sixth column. (In a very tight spot on a map or chart, *Cal., Col., Ia., Ida., Me. and Tex.* may be used.)

Alabama	AL	Ala.	Montana	MT	Mont.
Alaska	AK	Alaska	Nebraska	NE	Neb.
Arizona	AZ	Ariz.	Nevada	NV	Nev.
Arkansas	AR	Ark.	New Hampshire	NH	N.H.
California	CA	Calif.	New Jersey	NJ	N.J.
Colorado	CO	Colo.	New Mexico	NM	N.M.
Connecticut	CT	Conn.	New York	NY	N.Y.
Delaware	DE	Del.	North Carolina	NC	N.C.
District of Columbia	DC	D.C.	North Dakota	ND	N.D.
Florida	FL	Fla.	Ohio	OH	Ohio
Georgia	GA	Ga.	Oklahoma	OK	Okla.
Hawaii	HI	Hawaii	Oregon	OR	Ore.
Idaho	ID	Idaho	Pennsylvania	PA	Pa.
Illinois	IL	Ill.	Rhode Island	RI	R.I.
Indiana	IN	Ind.	South Carolina	SC	S.C.
Iowa	IA	Iowa	South Dakota	SD	S.D.
Kansas	KS	Kan.	Tennessee	TN	Tenn.
Kentucky	KY	Ky.	Texas	TX	Texas
Louisiana	LA	La.	Utah	UT	Utah
Maine	ME	Maine	Vermont	VT	Vt.
Maryland	MD	Md.	Virginia	VA	Va.
Massachusetts	MA	Mass.	Washington	WA	Wash.
Michigan	MI	Mich.	West Virginia	WV	W.Va.
Minnesota	MN	Minn.	Wisconsin	WI	Wis.
Mississippi	MS	Miss.	Wyoming	WY	Wyo.
Missouri	MO	Mo.			

(Kentucky, Massachusetts, Pennsylvania and Virginia are formally commonwealths but should be called states in all but legal references.) **See political regions.**

States, the. Capitalize when referring to the United States as a country: *on return to the States,* but *the states of the nation*.

staunch. **See stanch/staunch.**

Stealth. Unofficial name for the B-2A bomber and the F-117A fighter.

steelmaker

Steelworkers Union

stockholder, but *common-stock holder*

stocks and bonds. Use figures to indicate types of stocks and bonds: *sale of 2½s increased*.

storm. Capitalize when personified: *Tropical Storm Tessie (the tropical storm), Hurricane Hank*. Use *it*, not *she* or *he*.

Strategic Arms Limitation Treaty, but *strategic arms treaty, strategic arms limitation talks*. *SALT* is acceptable as a second reference to both the treaty and the talks. *SALT II*.

Street. Spell out and capitalize when part of an address. See addresses.

strongman

stubs. See charts and tables.

styles in the arts. See cultural designations.

sub( ). Combines solid except before a capital letter (*sub-Saharan*) or in Latin phrases, such as *sub judice*.

subcommittee. Capitalize in names of legislative groups: *the Senate Consumer and Regulatory Affairs Subcommittee (the Senate Consumer Affairs Subcommittee)*. Lowercase alone and when not the actual name: *the subcommittee, a Senate Banking subcommittee*. See committee.

subheads. Do not place subheads before the second paragraph of a story or directly before the kicker in a story.

such as. See like, as.

suffragist

summit conference. *the Clinton-Yeltsin summit conference (the summit)*.

sun. Lowercase except when personified: *the sun, a sun, suns, "Sisters of the Sun are gonna get down to the sea somehow."* See heavenly bodies.

Sun Belt

super( ). Combines solid except before capitalization or double word: *super aircraft carrier*, but *supercarrier*.

Super Bowl, *Super Bowl XXIV, the bowl*

superintendent. Capitalize before a name as a title; lowercase otherwise. Abbreviate, *supt.*, only in series, charts and maps.

Supreme Allied Commander Europe. Capitalize when used with a name, in exact form, as in *Rufus Fox, Supreme Allied Commander Europe,* but lowercase in altered form, as in *Rufus Fox, supreme allied commander for Europe*.

Supreme Court. *the U.S. Supreme Court (the Supreme Court, the court), the Arkansas Supreme Court (the state Supreme Court, the Supreme Court), a state's supreme court* (descriptive). Caution: *Supreme Court* does not always refer to a jurisdiction's highest court. The New York Supreme Court, for example, is a trial court; the highest court in New York is the Court of Appeals.

surgeon general. Capitalize before a name; lowercase otherwise: *Surgeon General Neal Deshpande (the surgeon general)*. Do not abbreviate.

symposium(s). Capitalize in an official name; lowercase otherwise: *the Hamburg symposium on protection of seacoasts against pollution, the Itinerant Symposium on the Granites of Northeast, the symposium*.

synagogue or temple. See Jewish congregations.

T

'I have tried to develop a personal style in my communications and my appearance that reflects well on U.S. News *and makes life a little easier for the reporters and editors here.'*

ALETHA TOWNSEND
TELEPHONE OPERATOR

table. Capitalize with a number or a letter: *Table 2, Table B*.

tables. See charts and tables.

take-home (noun and adjective): *How much is your take-home? I could use more take-home pay.*

Talmud

tanks. Write U.S. tank designations solid; hyphenate Russian designations. Follow the designations used in Jane's Armour: *M1, M2, M60A3* (U.S.), *T-34, T-54* (Russian), *AMX-30* (French).

(-)tax (adjective). *income-tax rise, property-tax payment*.

taxpayer, but *income-tax payer*

teachers college

teenage

teenager

telephone numbers. *(800) 555-1212, Ext. 501*. When the number is already in parentheses, or where space is tight in a chart or table, drop the parentheses around the area code and add a hyphen: *Phone home (215-682-1212) today*.

television. Quote the names of programs and the names of episodes but not the names of characters: *"Designing Women," "I Love Lucy,"* but *Lucy Ricardo*. *TV* is acceptable as an adjective on first reference and as a noun on second reference.

temperature. Use figures to indicate number of degrees. Except in tabular matter or series, spell out *degrees* and the designation of the scale being used. In tables or series, abbreviations or the degree symbol may be used: *7 degrees below zero Fahrenheit* (abbreviation: *–7°F*); *It was 10 below; a 15-degree difference; between 5 and 6 degrees Celsius* (abbreviation: *5° to 6°C*). See metric system.

temple or synagogue. See Jewish congregations.

Tennessean

Tennessee (Tenn., TN in addresses)

tenses. See hedging.

terrorism, terrorist. Limit the use of these words to politically motivated violent acts that are directed against noncombatants without regard for innocent lives. In a military context, *guerrilla* is a less politically loaded word to describe unconventional warfare. Write that people who admit such acts *take responsibility for* them, not that they *take credit for* them.

Texan

Texas (TX in addresses. Otherwise abbreviate, *Tex.,* only in a tight spot on a map, chart or table.)

that, which. Descriptive (nonrestrictive) clauses are set off by commas and take a "which": *The Band, which performed in Cambridge, has five members*. Defining (restrictive) clauses are not set off by commas and usually take a "that": *The band that played yesterday broke up today*.

the. See book titles, company names, newspapers.

theater, but follow a particular theater's spelling in a name: *Kreeger Theater, Ford's Theatre, the theater*.

then. *then President Ford, the then married couple*.

thin space is used to regularize spacing between certain elements and to keep intact elements that the computer would otherwise allow to break erroneously from one line to the next. For example, a thin space is used with subquotation marks and quotation marks (*"She said, 'Don't Go.' "*), with ellipses (*"They are married . . . with children"*) and with initials (*T. G. Shepherd*).

third. Use roman numerals after a name: *Robert Stein III*.

Third World

this week. It refers to the week preceding the cover date. So a person whose birthday falls during the week that begins with the cover date, for example, would be identified with the younger age. Each week begins on Monday and ends on Sunday.

time. Use figures for clock time (*3 p.m., 5:30 a.m., 6 o'clock*) and for hours, minutes, seconds, days, weeks, months and years greater than nine. Spell out for nine and less, except in reference to the age of an animate object (*She was 9 years old. She lived there nine years. She lived there 13 weeks*), when a fraction is connected to a whole number (*2½ hours*) or in combination with figures above nine (*The nurse spoke for 2 days and 13 hours*). Avoid such redundancies as *10 o'clock p.m.* and *12 noon*. Midnight is the end of a day, not the beginning. Don't use *12 a.m.* or *12 p.m.* Write *noon* or *midnight*.

time and a half. *He got paid time and a half. She received time-and-a-half pay.*

time elements. See hedging, this week.

times greater, times smaller. See greater than, as great as.

time zones. Capitalize the full name and abbreviate or spell out as appropriate: *Eastern Standard Time (EST), Eastern Daylight Time (EDT), Pacific Standard Time, Greenwich Mean Time,* but *the Eastern time zone, Eastern time, daylight-saving time. At 6:25 a.m. CST he left the hospital and drove home.*

titles of nobility. See nobility.

titles of persons. Capitalize titles when used as such before names; lowercase them when they follow the name, when they are used in apposition before a name, when they are standing alone and when qualifying words make them more descriptive than titular:

EXECUTIVE. *President Mason (the president); running for president; former President Ford (the former president); Italian President Aldo Troia,* but *Italy's president, Aldo Troia; Presidents Sanzone and Troia (the presidents); Premier Lee Groom (Premier Groom, the premier); Gov. Helen Davis (Governor Davis, the governor).*
ADMINISTRATIVE. *Secretary of State Hubert Shawker (the secretary of state, the secretary,* but *the Treasury secretary), Secretaries of State Shawker and Watson,*

Deputy Secretary of State Gaston Bornscheuer (the deputy secretary of state), U.S. Attorney General Robert Cooke (the attorney general), Secretary of the Navy Karol Weiss (the secretary of the Navy, the secretary), Foreign Minister Bruno Morowski (the foreign minister), Director of Central Intelligence Roy Tom (the director), Press Secretary Pam Gail (the press secretary), Chairman Darlene Lahey of the Federal Communications Commission (FCC Chairman Lahey, the FCC chairman).

LEGISLATIVE. *Sen. Robert Melville (Senator Melville, the senator); Rep. Marianne Sherwood (Representative Sherwood, the representative); House Majority Leader Satchmo Flinchum (Majority Leader Satchmo Flinchum, the majority leader); Holmes Elliott, president pro tem of the Senate; Speaker of the House Jan Stegman (House Speaker Jan Stegman, the speaker).*

JUDICIAL. *Chief Justice Emmylou Basham (the chief justice), Associate Justice Royd Luedde (Justice Royd Luedde, Justice Luedde, the associate justice, the justice), Chief Judge Roland Kelley (Judge Kelley, the chief judge, the judge).*

RELIGIOUS. *Pope John Paul II (Pope John Paul, the pope), the Rev. Betsy Haller.*

POLITICAL. *Democratic National Chairman Fred Manjone (Fred Manjone, the Democratic national chairman, the chairman).*

ROYALTY. *Princess Eleanor of Belgium (Princess Eleanor, the princess).*

BUSINESS. *Chief Executive Officer Blaine Mueller (the chief executive officer, the chief executive), Managing Editor Jesse Leedy (the managing editor, editor Leedy).*

OCCUPATIONAL DESCRIPTIONS are lowercase: *fashion designer Lauren Wenta; sports editor Glen Edgerton; first baseman Lou Gehrig,* but *Manager Miller Huggins; cellist Gregor Piatigorsky,* but *Conductor Arturo Toscanini*. When you encounter difficulty drawing the line between a title and an occupational description, a safe bet is to lowercase the description and put it after the name or set it off in apposition before the name with commas: *the paper's sports editor, Glen Edgerton, was honored*. When qualifying words make a title more a description than a title, the title may be spelled out and lowercased: *career ambassador Logan Winter, European-history professor Jill Farace, defeated Florida governor Bob Martinez, retired majority leader Sarah Collins,* but be consistent within an editorial package. Don't use double titles, such as *the Rev. Dr. Willy Wirtz*. See **military titles, Your Honor** and individual listings (**chair, pope, queen, senator,** etc.).

titles of works. Capitalize principal words and prepositions and conjunctions of more than three letters. For readability, make all-cap and all-lowercase titles caps and lowercase.

ITALICS. Put the following in italics, no quotes: titles of books, newspapers, magazines, newsletters, plays, movies, operas, oratorios and other long musical compositions with distinctive names, ballets, paintings, sculpture, computer programs, collections of poetry and long poems published separately.

QUOTATION MARKS. Put quotation marks around titles of short poems, essays, short stories, articles, pamphlets, booklets, lectures, speeches, dissertations, monographs, theses, reports, chapters, songs, radio and television programs, including made-for-television movies, and headlines.

ROMAN, NO QUOTES. Set in roman type, without quotation marks, titles of standard reference books, like dictionaries, almanacs and encyclopedias, and religious books, like the Bible and the Koran. **See book titles, computer programs, headlines, magazines, musical compositions, newspapers.**

ton. 2,000 pounds (short ton). Abbreviation, *t,* acceptable in charts and tables where the meaning is clear. Long ton (2,240 pounds) is used in Britain. **See metric ton.**

townhouse. A type of tall, narrow, usually attached dwelling, usually built in clusters in either the city or the suburbs.

town house. A city residence, usually so designated because the owner also has a place in the country.

toxin refers only to naturally produced substances. Do not use as a synonym for all toxic substances.

trademarks. A word or symbol used by a company to identify its goods or services, a trademark is legally protected from use by the owner's competitors and generally should not be lowercased or used in such a way that it seems to be a common noun, adjective or verb. Use a generic equivalent rather than a trademark unless a point is being made about a particular trademarked article or the trademark is deemed helpful in setting a scene. Thus for identity's sake we might write about a strike at a plant where Coca-Cola is bottled, but if we feel a brand reference is helpful when we write about "a labor dispute over operation of the Coke machine," we should (for accuracy's sake) be absolutely certain it is a Coke machine, and if we are not sure, we should describe it generically, as, for example, a "soft-drink machine" or a "vending machine." If trademarks are not guarded from use in senses that seem generic, they may officially lose protection of the law and can be employed thereafter by all companies. When this happens, there is no longer any restriction on writers. Former trademarks that have passed into the public domain: *aspirin, cellophane, cornflakes, cube steak, dry ice, escalator, kerosene, lanolin, linoleum, milk of magnesia, mimeograph, nylon, raisin bran, thermos, shredded wheat, touch-tone, trampoline, zipper*. As a good corporate citizen, *U.S. News,* which protects trademarks of its own, should strive to avoid misuse of other companies' trademarks. At the same time, we must be attuned to language evolution that turns hitherto-protected words into colorful and useful generic expressions. When you refer to a specific trademarked product, capitalize it: *Braise the trout in a Teflon skillet. They sold Band-Aids at the checkout counter.* When use of a brand name does not help the story or you are unsure of the brand, use a generic equivalent: *Braise the trout in a skillet with a nonstick coating. They sold adhesive bandages at the checkout counter.* Use a brand name generically only when such use is sanctioned by the dictionary: *She dubbed Reagan "the teflon president." The treasurer said the bill amounted to "nothing more than a band-aid solution to the problem."* Sources of information about trademarks, including new marks and others not listed in this entry:

1. Standard Directory of Advertisers
2. Style sheets of the United States Trademark Association. For telephone inquir-

ies: (212) 768-9886, daily 2 p.m. to 5 p.m.
3. For drugs, Physicians' Desk Reference

Trademark	**Generic**
A-1	sauce
Acrilan	acrylic fiber
Advil	ibuprofen pain reliever
Airfoam	sponge and cellular rubber
Anchor Fence	chain-link fence
Arnel	triacetate
AstroTurf	artificial turf
Aureomycin	antibiotic
Avril	rayon
Baggies	plastic bags
Band-Aid	adhesive bandage
Brillo	soap pad
Brown-in-Bag	oven bags
Celanese	acetate/nylon/polyester/rayon/triacetate
Chex	cereal
Chiclets	chewing gum
Chloromycetin	antibiotic
Clorox	bleach
Coca-Cola, Coke	soft drink, cola drink
Congoleum	floor coverings
Contac	antihistamine, decongestant
Cream of Wheat	cereal
Crisco	shortening
Cyclone	chain-link fence
Dacron	polyester fiber
Day-Glo	fluorescent paints, etc.
Deepfreeze	food freezer
Disposall	food-waste disposers
Dramamine	travel-sickness medicine
Dynel	modacrylic fiber
Electrolux	vacuum cleaner
Eveready	batteries
Fiberglas	fiberglass, glass fibers
Fig Newtons	cookies
Flit	insecticide
Formica	laminated plastic
Fortrel	polyester yarn
Frigidaire	refrigerator, appliances
Frisbee	plastic flying disk
Fritos	corn chips
Fudgsicle	ice cream on a stick
Gatorade	thirst quencher

Trademark	**Generic**
Gripper	snap fasteners
Hamburger Helper	packaged dinner mixes
Hawaiian Punch	fruit beverage
Jell-O	gelatin dessert
Jockey	underwear
Jonny Mop	toilet bowl cleaner
Kleenex	tissues
Kodachrome	film
Kodacolor	film
Kodak	film and cameras
Kodel	polyester
Kool-Aid	soft-drink mix
Kotex	sanitary napkins, belts, tampons
Lastex	elastic yarns
Levi's	jeans and sportswear
Liederkranz	cheese
Linotype	typesetting machine
Lucite	acrylic resin
Lycra	spandex fiber
Lysol	disinfectant
Mace	liquid tear-gas formulation
Masonite	hardboard products
Maypo	cereal
Mazola	margarine and corn oil
Mercurochrome	antiseptic
Miltown	tranquilizer
Minute	rice
Mixmaster	food mixer
Multilith	offset press
Muzak	music programs
Naugahyde	vinyl-coated fabrics
Neolite	composition soles and heels
Nescafé	instant coffee
Novocain	novocaine, anesthetic
Nutrament	food supplement
Orlon	acrylic fiber
Ouija	"talking board" sets
Oysterettes	crackers
Pablum	pabulum, baby cereal
Parcheesi	backgammon game
Pepsi-Cola, Pepsi	soft drink, cola drink
Photostat	photographic copy
Ping-Pong	table tennis equipment
Playtex	girdles and bras
Plexiglas	acrylic plastic

Trademark	Generic
Polaroid	photographic equipment
Polaroid	polarizing sunglasses
Popsicle	frozen confection
Post Toasties	cereal
Postum	cereal beverage
Prestone	antifreeze
Pyrex	heat-resistant glassware
Q-Tips	cotton swabs
Realtor	real-estate broker, agent, specialist
Ritz	crackers
Rollerblades	in-line skates
Sanforized	compressively shrunk fabric
Scotch	cellophane tape
Scrabble	word game
7-Up	soft drink
Sheetrock	gypsum wallboard
Styrofoam	plastic foam
Sucaryl	sweetener
Sunbeam	appliances
Sunkist	fruit and juices
Tabasco	sauce
Technicolor	motion-picture color process
Teflon	fluorocarbon resins
TelePrompTer	cuing apparatus
Teletype	teletypewriter and other equipment
Teletypesetter	telegraphic typesetting machine
Terramycin	antibiotic
Thermo-Fax	copying machines
Thiokol	liquid polymers
Thorazine	tranquilizer
Tinkertoy	construction toy
Toastmaster	electric appliances
Tylenol	acetaminophen pain reliever
Unicap	vitamins
Vaseline	petroleum jelly, hair tonic
Velcro	hook-and-loop fastener, touch fastener
Videoscan	document reader
Vycron	polyester
Xerox	xerographic copiers
Zepel	fabric water repellent
Zerex	antifreeze
ZipNut	push-on nut

See adrenalin, jeep.

trans( ). Combines solid except before capitalization: *transmundane, trans-Atlantic*.

Treasury. *Treasury bills, Treasuries, T-bills, Secretary of the Treasury Ariel Hicks, Treasury Secretary Hicks (secretary of the Treasury, the Treasury secretary).*

treaty. Capitalize as part of an official name; lowercase alone: *Treaty of Versailles (Versailles Treaty, the treaty).* See the electronic NAMES list.

trillion. See million.

tropical storm. *Tropical Storm Wendy (the tropical storm);* use *it*, not *her* or *him*.

turned. Do not hyphenate such constructions as *editor turned plumber*.

TV. Acceptable as an adjective on first reference; acceptable as a noun on second reference.

twin-engine (adjective)

two-by-four (noun and adjective)

(-)type. Hyphenate when used as an adjective meaning "of that sort": *a Western-type saddle,* but *He was a Hollywood type*.

typhoid, typhus. Typhoid (fever) is a salmonella-caused disease; typhus is a disease caused by bites from fleas or lice.

U

'Reporting, whether financial or otherwise, requires a descriptive, analytical mind, attention to detail and a great sense of humor.'

PECK KIM UNG
SENIOR ACCOUNTANT

ultra( ). Combines solid except before a capital letter or an *a.*

un( ). Combines solid except before a capital letter.

U.N. Acceptable after first reference to United Nations. See United Nations.

under( ). Generally combines solid except before capitalization, but *under secretary.*

under secretary. Capitalize as a title before a name; lowercase otherwise: *Under Secretary of State Carol Stroll (the under secretary of state, the under secretary).*

understrength

union. Capitalize when it refers to the Northern states during the Civil War: *the states of the Union.*

union names. Capitalize *union* when it is part of a labor union name or a paraphrase thereof; lowercase otherwise: *Teamsters Union, United Automobile, Aerospace and Agricultural Implement Workers of America (United Auto Workers Union, United Auto Workers, the auto union, the union).* Follow union style on use of apostrophes: *International Ladies' Garment Workers Union, Directors Guild of America.* Use *and,* not an ampersand, in union names.

United Methodist Church. Some nonordained persons serve in special capacities as deacons. They may be described as such but are not officially referred to by a title or an honorific like *the Rev.* When a layperson "supplies" a church (serves it as pastor), it is a customary courtesy to put *the Rev.* before the person's name. Ordained persons first become deacons, then elders. All ordained persons are referred to as *the Rev.* Either a deacon or an elder may be a pastor; to hold a position higher than pastor, one must be an elder. All titles are used for men and women alike. Women as well as men can be deacons, pastors and bishops. *Tenth Street United Methodist Church (the church), the Rev. Harwood Johnson, pastor of Tenth Street United Methodist Church (the pastor, Johnson), Bishop Harwood Johnson of the Kentucky Area (Bishop Johnson, the bishop, Johnson).*

United Nations (U.N.). *United Nations Charter (the charter), Security Council (the council), General Assembly (the Assembly), Secretary General Robert Cooke (the secretary general, the secretariat).*

United States (U.S., U.S.A.). *the States* (referring to the nation), *the states* (referring to the individual states). Do not abbreviate when used as a noun, except in quotes. The possessive is *United States'*. See we.

university. Capitalize in a name; lowercase alone: *Brigham Young University (the university)*. See colleges and universities.

upper. See central.

up-to-dateness. The need to take note of the latest, in large concerns or small, goes beyond legal cases. The problem is not only that a case may have been dismissed, deferred or appealed. Bills in a legislature may have been passed or defeated, lost people may have been found, feuding politicians may have made up, local prices may have risen, building projects may have been abandoned. And even if our story was correct when written yesterday, something may have happened since. Both the writer and the editors must spot those things that could change and keep watch over them until publication.

us. See we.

USA. Acceptable, when clear, for references to the United States Army.

U.S.A. See United States.

USAF. Acceptable, when clear, for references to the United States Air Force.

U.S. attorney. Capitalize before a name; lowercase otherwise. Keep the *U.S.* after first reference or use another word, like *prosecutor,* to avoid confusion.

USMC. Acceptable, when clear, for references to the United States Marine Corps.

USN: *United States Navy, U.S. Navy*. USNR: *United States Naval Reserve, U.S. Naval Reserve*.

USN&WR (italicized). Abbreviation used in credits.

U.S. News (italicized) is for general use of the name. Put a space between ***U.S.*** and ***News***. For the formal name, ***U.S.News & World Report***, use no space between ***U.S.*** and ***News***.

USS (United States Ship)

Utah (UT in addresses; do not abbreviate otherwise)

Utahan is an adjective meaning of or from Utah. *Utahn* is a noun meaning a resident of Utah.

utopian

V

'A copy editor needs a picky eye for detail, a thick skin and, above all, a good sense of humor. It's the only way to keep your sanity when two hours' worth of editing crashes.'

SUSAN BURLANT VAVRICK
NEWS EDITOR

v. Use, italicized, for *versus* in legal citations: ***Jones v. NLRB***. See vs.

VA. Acceptable on second reference to the Department of Veterans Affairs.

valley. Capitalize when part of a real or fanciful name; lowercase otherwise: *Red River Valley, Silicon Valley, Happy Valley (the valley)*.

van. See particles.

VCR. Acceptable on second reference to *videocassette recorder*.

VDT. Acceptable, when clear, on second reference to *video display terminal*.

veep

venetian. *venetian red, venetian blinds,* but *Venetian glass* (made in or near Venice).

verbal. See oral/verbal.

Vermont (Vt., VT in addresses)

Vermonter

verse. Run lines together, separated by thin spaces on both sides of a virgule: *He thought it happier to be dead, / To die for beauty, than live for bread.*

versus. Use ***v.*** for court citations; otherwise, *versus* and *vs.* are acceptable.

Very Rev. See Episcopal Church, Roman Catholic Church.

Veterans Day

vice. *vice admiral, vice chairman, vice president, vice regent, viceroy, vice squad.*

vice presidency

vice president. Capitalize before a name; lowercase otherwise: *Vice President Jon Baron (the vice president).* First names of American vice presidents need not be used on first reference with the title unless confusion would otherwise result.

vice presidential

vice/vise. Vice is evil or wicked conduct; a vise means a firm grip or a tool.

victim. Keep in mind that some people consider the word sensational in such uses as *a polio victim, an AIDS victim.* People with such conditions generally do not like language that suggests their lives are tragic or to be pitied. Preferred are such constructions as *a person with polio. Victim* is found offensive because these people do not see themselves as victims, nor do they want to be seen as victims. Likewise, the use of *patient* for people who are not hospitalized or undergoing treatment is considered offensive because it suggests someone to be pitied, when a person with cerebral palsy or a similar condition may in fact be in otherwise excellent health and live a long life. See disabled, handicap.

video. *video arcade, video camera, video display terminal, video game, video programs, videotape recording, videocassette, videocassette recorder, videodisc.*

Virginia (Va., VA in addresses)

Virginian

Virgin Islands (V.I., VI in addresses). Inhabitants are *residents of the Virgin Islands.*

vitamin. *vitamin A, vitamin* B_{12}.

voice. See active voice.

von. See particles.

vote getter

vote tabulations. Use figures: *The clean-air bill was approved 347 to 29. A 347-to-29 margin* or, where space is at a premium, as in headlines and captions, *a 347-29 margin*.

vs. Acceptable abbreviation for *versus,* except in legal citations, where it is ***v.*** Both letters are lowercase, except in the unlikely event *vs.* begins a sentence or a headline, in which case it is *Vs.* See v.

vulgarity. See obscenity, profanity, vulgarity.

VW. Acceptable for Volkswagen on second reference.

W

' "Whoever knew truth put to the worse in a free and open encounter [with falsehood]?" John Milton wrote. One wonders how Milton would react to the White House propaganda machine.'

KENNETH T. WALSH
SENIOR WHITE HOUSE CORRESPONDENT

wall, the. When used as a nickname for a structure whose name does not include the word *wall,* such as the Vietnam Veterans Memorial, put the first such reference in quotation marks (*It was Ken's first visit to "the wall"*). But when used alone to refer to a structure with *wall* in its name, write it lowercase, without quotation marks: *Ellen clutched a piece of the Berlin Wall (the wall).*

wangle/wrangle. Wangle means to bring about by persuasion or trickery; wrangle means to quarrel angrily and noisily, or to herd.

wannabe(s). Acceptable as a noun when context makes the meaning clear. For adjectival use, *would-be* is better.

war. Capitalize in names of past and current wars; lowercase alone: *the Korean War (the war), Spanish Civil War, Vietnam War, World War I, the First World War, World War II, the Second World War, World War III, the next world war, a world war, the world wars, Yom Kippur War, the Civil War (U.S.),* but *the civil war in Lebanon, Lebanese civil war (Lebanese Civil War* if it becomes historically so known), *cold war*. See the electronic NAMES list.

War Between the States. Used as a reference to the U.S. Civil War by those sympathetic to the Confederacy.

ward. Capitalize in a name; lowercase alone: *Fourth Ward, 16th Ward (the ward).*

war front

war maker

warrant officer. See military titles.

Washington (Wash., WA in addresses). When there is the possibility of confusion with Washington, D.C., write *Washington State* or *the state of Washington*.

Washington, D.C. (do not abbreviate *Washington*). *D.C.* is not necessary as long as there is no possibility of confusion with Washington State.

Washingtonian. A resident of the state of Washington or of the District of Columbia.

waste water

( )watcher. *China watcher, China watching,* but *bird-watcher* and *bird-watching*.

we. In general, avoid using first-person singular and plural. Except in columns and editorials, do not use *we, us, our* and *ours* when referring to the United States or the American people.

weapons. Jane's Weapon Systems is a helpful guide, but note some cases in which *U.S. News* style varies from Jane's. The examples that follow are not intended to dictate descriptive terms. For instance, the 7.3-mm weapon does not have to be called a pistol. If it is an automatic, it may be so designated: *12-gauge shotgun, .410-bore shotgun* (the .410 is actually caliber), *.22-caliber rifle, .30-30 rifle* (.30 caliber, 30 grains of powder in cartridge), *M-16 rifle, .45-caliber automatic, .32-caliber revolver, 7.3-mm pistol, M-60 machine gun, 75-mm gun, .50-caliber machine gun, .357-caliber Magnum*. Generally, a semiautomatic weapon is one that fires each time the trigger is pulled and an automatic is one that continues to fire as long as the trigger is held. However, pistols that fire either automatically or seimautomatically are usually called *automatics.* A bullet is the projectile fired by a gun or rifle; a cartridge consists of the bullet and its primer, propellant and casing.

weather phenomena. Capitalize when personified: *Hurricane Tessie (the hurricane), Tropical Storm Henry (the tropical storm)*. Use *it,* not *he* or *she*.

week. Capitalize in the name of a specially designated period: *Holy Week, National Safety Week.*

weeklong

week, this. See this week.

weights and measures. Use figures: *13 inches; 6 pounds; 9 miles; 120 volts; she was 5 feet, 2 inches tall; a 5-foot, 2-inch woman*.
ABBREVIATIONS. *Btu, mpg* and *mph* may be used on all references in an article if the meaning is clear. *Hp, psi* and *rpm* may be used on second reference in an article. The other abbreviations should be used only in charts, maps and tables. Singular abbreviations are both singular and plural.

barrel(s)	bbl.
British thermal unit(s)	Btu
bushel(s)	bu
calorie(s)	cal.
dollar(s)	$
foot (feet)	ft.
gallon(s)	gal.
horsepower	hp
hour(s)	hr.
inch(es)	in.
mile(s)	mi.
miles per gallon	mpg
miles per hour	mph
minute(s)	min.
ounce(s)	oz.
pound(s)	lb.
pounds per square inch	psi
quarter	qtr., q.
revolutions per minute	rpm
second(s)	sec.
ton(s)	t.
yard(s)	yd.
year(s)	yr.

See metric system, numbers, time.

well(-). When combining with an adjective before a noun, hyphenate: *well-prepared student, well-versed writer, well-known actor,* but *very well known actor*. When the combination is used after the noun, drop the hyphen unless the result would be confusing: *He was well preserved. Her back was well massaged. The compliment was well deserved*.

west, western. Capitalize in a name or when they designate a region; lowercase when merely a direction: *driving out West* (but *driving west*), *the Old West, West Coast, Western world, Western Europe, Western Hemisphere, Western states, Western movie (a Western), Westerner, West End* (of London), but *westbound, western pine, western omelet, country-and-western music, westernize*. **See compass directions.**

Western allies, but the *Allies* and *Allied powers* in World War II. **See Allies, Allied.**

West Virginia (W.Va., WV in addresses)

West Virginian

wheelchairbound. Disabled people find terms such as this and "confined to a wheelchair" offensive, believing that they generally exaggerate one's inability. Except for extreme cases of quadriplegia, people can get in and out of wheelchairs, usually by themselves. We would not write "eyeglassbound." Preferred terminology includes: *uses a wheelchair, a wheelchair user*.

which. See that, which.

whip. Capitalize as a title before a name; lowercase otherwise.

whiskey(s)/whisky(whiskies). Use *whisky* for *Scotch whisky* and *Canadian whisky*. Use *whiskey* for all other references: *bourbon whiskey, rye whiskey, whiskey sour*.

white paper. Lowercase unless part of a name.

who/whom. Perhaps *whom* will someday bite the dust, but until it does, use it properly: *Whom do you trust?* (*whom* is the object of the verb *trust*). *Who is going to the dance?* (*who* is the subject). *Who shall I say called?* (*who* is the subject). *The friends whom Peter framed were set free* (*whom* is the object of *framed*). *The friends who Manny said were present signed up* (*who* is the subject, hidden from its verb, *were,* by *Manny said*).

( )wide. Combines solid: *citywide, companywide, countrywide, industrywide, nationwide, plantwide, statewide, worldwide*.

wife, husband. Use commas: *Bob brought his wife, Melissa, home* (unless he has more than one wife).

windfall-profits tax

Wisconsin (Wis., WI in addresses)

Wisconsinite

( )wise. When the word denotes a way or manner, it usually combines solid: *lengthwise*. Meaning sage, it usually takes a hyphen: *penny-wise*.

( ) word. If you must use such expressions as *the "L" word,* put the letter in quotation marks.

words as words. Italicize: *He inserted an* ***and*** *into the record.*

workday. A day on which work is done.

work-day. A measure of the amount of work a person does in one day.

( )worker. Usually solid when the term describes a person working in a certain material, two words when it concerns a person working on an object or in a place: *auto worker, factory worker, farm-implement worker, farm worker, ironworker, metalworker, mine worker, office worker, steelworker*.

workers' compensation. Use plural even if only one person is involved: *She filed for workers' compensation, a workers' compensation suit.*

work force

work-hour. A measure of the amount of work a person does in one hour.

workplace

works of art. Use italics: *Michelangelo's* ***Madonna of the Stairs***. See titles of works.

workweek

world. *the world, Western world, Third World, New World, Old World*. See compass directions.

World Bank. Customary reference to the International Bank for Reconstruction and Development.

World Community of Islam in the West. See Islam.

World Series. *the Series*.

( )worthy. Usually combines solid: *airworthy*.

wrack. See rack.

wrangle. See wangle/wrangle.

Wyoming (Wyo., WY in addresses)

Wyomingite

XYZ

'Uh, that's with two N's, please; my mother's going to read this.'

TIM ZIMMERMANN
FOREIGN AFFAIRS REPORTER

x. When it stands for an unknown quantity, make it italic and lowercase: ***x** dollars*. Capitalize references to the former film rating: *movie rated X, an X-rated movie*.

X-ray

yard(s). Abbreviation, *yd.,* acceptable only in charts, maps and tables.

year. Abbreviation, *yr.,* acceptable only in charts, maps and tables. Use figures: *1964, 1964-66, the 1960s, the '60s, the 1800s, mid-'90s, March 1988,* but spell out decades when appropriate to the context: *Roaring Twenties, lost in the Fifties*. See ages, dates, decades.

yellow pages. When used to mean a directory, it takes a singular verb.

yes. Capitalize if in quotes: *The answer is "Yes."* But *The answer is yes.*

yet. When it means *and* or *but,* it is a conjunction; when it means *nevertheless,* it is an adverb and should usually be followed by a comma.

young turk. Capitalize when referring to members of the early-20th-century Turkish revolutionary group; lowercase when referring to insurgents seeking to take power from an older group.

Your Honor, etc. Capitalize *Your Majesty, Her Majesty, Your Grace, Your Excellency, Your Honor, Her Royal Highness, His Eminence,* etc. Lowercase *my lord*. Use them all only when quoting someone.

ZIP code. In addresses, use no comma between the state abbreviation and the ZIP code: *711 Keeley Street, Chicago, IL 60608*. Five-digit ZIP codes are usually sufficient, but when writing nine-digit ZIP codes, as on the contents page, use a hyphen: *2400 N Street, N.W., Washington, DC 20037-1196.*

ORDERING INFORMATION

Copies of the wirebound U.S.News & World Report Stylebook for Writers and Editors *are available in the United States for $10.55 plus $2.95 shipping. Please send check or money order to: Stylebook, U.S.News & World Report, Department CGB, 2400 N Street, N.W., Washington, DC 20037-1196. For credit card orders, please call (202) 955-2396. Rates for bulk orders are available on request. Please allow three to four weeks for delivery.* U.S. News *donates a portion of its stylebook profits to American literacy programs.*